Reaching for Greater Glory

Getting Through Unforeseen Storms and Pain Gracefully

By

Aminga Burton-Bracy

ISBN: 978-1-4033-6639-9 (sc)
ISBN: 978-1-4033-6638-2 (e)

Print information available on the last page.

This book is printed on acid-free paper.

Publisher: 1stBooks Library
1663 Liberty Drive, Bloomington, IN 47403

Editor: Dr. Benson Prigg
Cover Design: Seitu King

1stBooks - rev. 09/25/2020

In loving memory of my late Father,
Mr. Coleridge Burton

ACKNOWLEDGEMENT

Thanks to God, my highest source of power, for planting the gift of writing within me. A special thanks to my mom, Velva Burton, for investing in my education as well as for being my spiritual rock, prayer warrior, and setting a high standard entrepreneurially and morally. Kudos to my husband, Marvin Bracy, for supporting my dreams and being a great husband and father. Thanks to my son, Mikhail, for being my extraordinary teacher and helping me keep things in the right perspective; you are my biggest blessing from God.

This book would not be possible without a few good people: Dr. Benson Prigg, PhD (Editor), Lee Charles (Poet/*Ebony Magazine* contributor), Dr. Ben Okanume (Author & Writing Coach), and Seitu King (Graphic Designer). Also, I thank my family and friends who supported and prayed for me over the years.

CONTENTS

INTRODUCTION

For years, like millions of people around the world, I was groping around in darkness searching for answers I could not find to some of life's most basic questions. Like most, I would wake up each day thinking I found the answer to discover the champion within me and believing it was the moment I would begin to live life to the fullest. When in fact I was only gradually becoming more self-absorbed and alienating myself from God, the restorative source and give of love, peace, and happiness. In those self-absorbed moments the more I tried to achieve success the more dis-ease and discontent I felt. Just when I thought I had found the secret to success I would have a revolving door experience, ending up right where I started. Eventually, I started to think it was normal because it happens to most people I knew. I just simply wanted to live the American dream. However, one day reality hit home and I realized I was searching for answers in all the wrong places.

What I was searching for was glorious living, to live life to the fullest—finding love, joy, peace, and happiness in job security, money, friends, and family. Instead, I found emptiness and discontent. I sought solace in the one thing I am good at, my work ethic. After "bouncing" around in corporate America—from Fortune 500 Company to Government to Non-profit to faith-based organizations—trying to find the right job-fit I soon came to realize that no matter how hefty the compensations offered it did not bring adequate levels of peace, hope, and harmony I was craving. Although at times the payoff, from one job to the next, was seemingly beneficial I was uncomfortable and miserable doing some of the tasks most equated to gaining the competitive advantage. My aim was climbing the ladder of corporate success, but no matter how hard I worked there was always somebody craftier than me, not necessarily in work ethics.

Finally, I realized that I cannot live life to the fullest without God's glory. This is something we cannot acquire in ourselves; it comes from oneness with our Creator. After this realization, I struggled watching others strive to attain glory in their own strength. I shrug when I see people compromise their own standards—cheating, lying, manipulating others, corporate greed, uncaring, and workplace bullying—trying to get their way. Many so adamantly seek self-gratification they are not even cognizant of the consequences of their actions. This is even more prevalent in today's social media era where people are searching desperately to compete they'll do just about anything for the hype of a 'like'. But, is it really worth it? While moments of self-gratification makes us feel instantly fulfilled and may even bring some monetary compensations, those moment of glory which gets us one step above the competition are not lasting and may have lasting consequences. We'll have to keeping digging into our bag of tricks until eventually, we have a crash landing.

In a human context, glorious living is achievable in the absence of manipulations or self-stimulation. It's those moments we feel loved, hopeful, peaceful, and joyous after the lights go out, the media is turned off, and no one is around. What people conceive as glorious living is usually those momentary pleasures enjoyed when indulging, while imposing on others to get ahead, and Godly principles we abandon to achieve either or both. These momentary indulgences are also what obscures glorious living and leaves us feeling miserable, empty, inferior, sad, and incomplete.

Most people today reject the notion that wrong doing is sin and yield because the rewards are felt immediately for those who indulge and enjoy its present gratification. Many hide behind the notion that "everyone is doing it" or "it feels good" using it as confirmation of right and walk around masking their pain and concealing our emptiness from others so that even those closest to us maybe clueless about their actions and pain. We successfully fool ourselves into thinking we are not that bad, especially when it is popular. Sometimes we reject religion, using it as an excuse to impose on others and indulge ourselves, but we only fool ourselves because God knows what's in their hearts and judge our actions. Humanity rarely gets away with wrongs-doing no matter how gifted we are at masking. Sooner or later and in one way or another, people who indulge in wrongs fall victim. Scientifically, this consistent with Sir Isaac Newton's law of gravity, *"What goes up must come down"*. Spiritually, there is a biblical connotation, which states: *"for what a man sow—that he shall reap"* (Gal. 6: 7; YLT). To look beyond our immediate temporal benefits and contemplate on the long-term consequences of our actions go beyond temporal gains and in the end results in lasting fulfillment and enjoy glorious living.

A simple analogy, based on my personal experience, is depicted in my quest for glorious living. A desire to live gloriously kept me working a typical 8:00 to 5:00 job over the years even with a Masters degree. I was hoping for my momentary breakthrough in corporate work and kept working faithfully day after day trying to make a difference in a dubious work climate where sabotage was seemingly the work ethic of the day. Even while looking for a way out, I kept search for answers within my own limited scope and while I received some temporal benefits I was unhappy and uncomfortable because I was not fulfilling God's purpose for my life and wasn't aligning my life for glorious living. However, as I begin to reach God began to work behind the scene using His unique approach and timing to align me for lasting fulfillment. Once I recognize this, I begin to reject the temporal means of advancing myself and yield. I realized the temporal momentary measures were only limiting me and robbing me of the freedom of walking in God purpose.

Yielding to God and denying temporal gratifications that lead to consequences, God began to unveil His true plan and purpose for my life. This is not activated by works, but faith in God. Strangely enough, by I began to realize God was using this experience as my training ground to develop my character in preparation for something not even I could conceive. Living right is not always easy and is not strewn with roses, but it has lasting satisfaction that supersede even the greatest intensity of difficulties I face in life.

Although I am still a work-in-progress, which all began years ago, until God began to reveal Himself to me and unveil His purpose and plan for my life I had no clue about glorious living. I do not know which way life will take me but as I deny myself each day and trust the spirit it gives me a sense of purpose. I found that living life to the fullest is synonymous with glorious living which comes with love, joy, peace, and harmony with the Creator. Before, my concept of glorious living was obscured by the human limits—manipulations or self-stimulation. As I continue to be a work-in-progress (God's workmanship; Eph. 2:10), giving up my selfish pursuits and trusting God totally without leaning to my own understanding, is my daily goal. In the absence of this, I would have never known what glorious living was really about. Glorious living is not the absence of real life problems, but our ability to rise above them and not allow obscured moments to cloud out the love, joy, peace, and happiness.

Glorious living does not happen in a vacuum; it comes as a result of living a life where God rules and reigns in our lives. It does not happen overnight. For me, this process began years ago when I woke up to a probing Spirit. I wasn't sure what it was at the time, but over time I learned it was what is known scripturally as the Holy Spirit. Like most people I ignored that subtle voice within but it kept getting louder and louder, not in a literal sense but stronger in its probing. Once I began to pay attention to these probing things in my life became clearer and makes more sense. That voice has led me to begin uncovering that I have a higher calling. Although I cannot see all God has in store for me to many inconceivable places over the years and has prevented me from making life-altering mistakes. Some may say it's a coincidence, but I believe it is how the Master designs our destiny; He who originates glory:

love, joy, peace, hope, and harmony. Over the years, God reveals Himself to me in various ways; sometimes, so subtle that if I do not block out the

As human, we are born intrinsically with selfish tendencies which can be overcome but not in our own strength. We serve a God who is unimpressed by our outward manifestations—appearances, expressions, and materializations—but a God who wants us to prosper: emotionally, mentally, physically, socially, and spiritually. The more we indulge to make ourselves look great in others eyes, the more we are alienated from God who wants to help us find our place in this world. Finding our place is crucial to glorious living, which is fully within reach. Glorious living is not temporal; it is lasting and the only type of glory accessible to us on earth. Only those who reach will become recipients.

Although glorious living is within reach, we cannot activate it ourselves. Reaching requires giving up some things we cherish, anything not aligned to glorious living including friends, job, money, security, spouse, petty jealousies, etc. This is never easy. Reaching entails detachment, which may be tough and why most people fail. Cecil Parker, on a poster I saw years ago, captures this concept perfectly by indicating: *"the turtle can only move forward by first sticking out its neck."* By denying ourselves and detaching from people or things that don't align with God's purpose for our lives, we stick out our necks and activate faith which enables God's true purpose for our lives. Each time we practice self-denial and detachment from things we hold dear, our character is strengthened.

No matter what today's norms may be, reaching warrants letting go of wrongdoings in our lives. It's so much easier to look at others wrongdoings than to see our own faults. In a lecture series Dr. Robert Sternberg, a renowned psychologist, expressed that some people have a tendency to see themselves through rose colored glasses but see others through a magnifying glass. Reaching calls for looking away from others and focusing on ourselves, seeing how God sees us. Today, we are overly obsessed with ourselves and how others see us. Being overly concerned about others perceptions of us—while it matters in the smaller scheme of things—only stifles our creativity, authenticity, and uniqueness. If we allow our minds to become obscured by others point of view, it is difficult to see God's plan and purpose for our lives. Letting go of our inhibitions, God reveals His truth and plan for our lives. God never misleads us.

Reaching calls for opening up and choosing not to look back on what could have or should have been but on what God is doing to change our lives positively. Such a change brings wholeness that can withstand pending storms and pain we encounter in our lives. Storms—anything disruptive in our lives physically, economical, mentally, socially—will come in various ways but people who reach for greater glory will never be defeated. Continual reaching advances one's progress.

Wouldn't you like to wake up one morning knowing you and your family will have lasting fulfillment that transcend difficult circumstances? Would you like to reduce stress in your life or answer to no one but God and yourself? Would you like to live your life to the fullest despite the uncontrollable and unexpected storms to live free and happy? This is glorious living which is not impossible, and it may surprise you just how easy it is. It's much simpler than you may think. By taking a proactive look at the tools conveyed in this book, you will be well on your way to discovering the champion within, unleashing God's true purpose and plan for your life, and living gloriously. Riches and popularity are not guaranteed but you'll experience something more rewarding and lasting: love, joy, peace, hope and harmony. These are things associated with permanent glory, something not easily attainable outside the presence of God and will not be destroyed easily unless you step outside the environment where ultimate Glory.

Reaching for Greater Glory is an inspirational and informative book which helps readers grasp what transpired in Eden, understand how it impacts them now and the promises of hope it holds for the future.

YLT (Young's Literal Translation)

Chapter 1

ORIGIN OF LOST GLORY

Adam was in the Garden of Eden partaking of the radiance of God's glory—joy, peace and harmony he shared with Eve shortly before she wondered off into an environment where sin reigned; for where sin reigns, glory cannot abound. Somehow, the allurement of the serpent was stronger than Eve's desire to obey, and she suddenly lost her glory. After Adam partook of the forbidden fruit of Eve's dishonor with her, he too lost his glory. For the first time, Adam understood what fear meant; he suddenly became afraid of His Creator in a way that he never was prior to partaking of the forbidden fruit. Without any form of confrontation by God, Adam and Eve gradually began to wander away from the paths of righteousness. Slowly, they drifted through the wilderness deeper and deeper into the enemy's territory. Their separation and walking away from God's full glory left them naked and longing for the Creator.

That's precisely what sin does to us. It puts us in an environment that makes us uncomfortable and afraid to confront God, our loved ones and our friends not because of anything that they had done to us but as the adage goes, "a guilty conscience needs no accusers." Guilt results immediately when one yields to any circumstance that leads to a severed relationship with the Creator. Adam and Eve initiated a death that humanity has sought to manipulate throughout history.

Humanity has lost glory. If there is any chance of getting it back, we have to resist our sins and see the error of our ways. Oftentimes, we see only big things as sin, but the Bible tells us that "If we offend in even one of the least of God's commandments we are guilty of all" (James 2:10). As small as one disobedient act seems, it was enough for Adam and Eve to lose their glory. Today, you and I are still paying the price for choices Adam and Eve made, yet we have the options to submit or resist the will of the creator. When we sin, we pay a price—a penalty, consequences or repercussions for the bad choices we make, but just as how God went looking for Adam and Eve, He still comes looking for us even when we are skeptical or indifferent. God always comes down to our level as well as reaches out to us in love and mercy when we can't face Him; He wants us to have what is rightfully ours, glorious living, in spite of our inglorious behavior.

Glory is the temporal brightness we feel in our lives that makes us feel innate joy, hope, peace and harmony when surrounded by God's presence. When God's glory is in our lives, we can break forth into an explosion of joy, hope, comfort and peace each day. This glory makes us come fully alive bursting forth radiantly because we are at peace with being in harmony with the Creator. This comes by being at one with Him through spiritual, natural, and social laws. Being in harmony with these God-given laws in all three realms puts each of us in a position to act alive as a person. This position of existence does not come from someone else, so no one else can take it away unless we yield the position to him.

Glorious experience comes to us as temporary blessings and leaves as soon as we enter into an environment that is not conducive for God to coexist in. The challenge is to have sustained moments of blessings while often experiencing seen and unforeseen crises. Such crises are often viewed as problems, which prevent growth rather than as possibilities to produce growth. Once we see the potential of growth in the midst of a crisis, we may begin to yearn for an environment where our Creator is always present. As we draw back into the realm where God's presence can be felt, we feel a temporary glory that keeps us wanting to have it back when we wander away from it. It is like being in a loving relationship then something disrupts the love until we realize what is at stake, and we make up with our partner; the end result of the making up is such a joy we desire no more break ups. What begins this restoration process to return and stay in the presence of the Creator is an empowering Spirit who will lead us as we go through the crisis, "an opportunity cleverly disguised as a problem," of this world and fill us with glory. If we consistently strive for that mark, even when we are undergoing certain difficulties, we can experience something wonderfully grand down here that leads to ultimate glory, beholding the second coming of Him with whom we will spend eternity with.

In ultimate glory, humanity was an earthly image of the joy, peace and harmony in the spiritual realm until evil manifested itself. Our first parents knew of the ultimate glory as they walked in the presence of the Creator, who also walked in the presence of

His creatures. But something went terribly wrong. Something disrupted their Edenic lifestyle; their joy, peace and harmony with the Creator's spiritual, natural, and social laws. The relationship between Adam, Eve and the Creator was severed resulting in a death. The father of evil, once known as Lucifer the highest angel next to the Divine Creator, interrupted the glorious flow of humanity's first parents. Lucifer effectively deceived Eve and Adam causing them to disregard God's request hence spiritual death. This external source of temptation to eat for pleasure rather than for nourishment resulted in death and caused our first parents to be ashamed of each other, hence social death. While physical death was not immediate, turning away from the spiritual, natural and human social laws resulted in a death, a blemishing, and a cutting off from ultimate glory—perfect joy, peace and harmony with God the Creator.

Since that time, humanity has been tainted, tarnished, and taunted with the darkness of Satan's gloom. We have become overshadowed with the guilt from the sting of sin that causes us to feel vulnerable, sad, fearful, anxious and easily terrified. "Because *all* have sinned and fall short of the glory of God" (Romans 3:23), He has placed enmity (Genesis 3:15) between Satan and Eve's seed, humanity, to create discomfort when in an ambiance of evil thus causing us to desire that which is right. This enmity is the source of our desire to find the greater glory that some of us may never regain even though there are opportunities when it can be regained.

Though we are formed in sin and shaped in iniquity within the womb, we are most prone to achieve glory until something, usually the baggage or hang-ups, disrupts our desire for attaining glory. Another opportunity that makes us desirous of reclaiming our full glory involves our human spirit yielding to the Holy Spirit's voice; thus, there is a "born again experience." Additionally, when in a lifestyle that actively responds to the Spirit's voice, we must stop fighting the Voice and yield to it. These points of returning to God are moments that He may bring back our glory though it may be limited while on this earth. Yet, even the father of Evil knows that once we get a taste of glory, we will want a full measure of it as our first parents once experienced.

There are three things that happened back in the Garden of Eden that still has a profound impact on humanity today evident in our wandering, sin and lost glory. Although wandering wasn't a sin, it wasn't the best choice that Eve made. It caused her to end up on enemy territory where she became vulnerable to Satan's deceptions. However innocent it seems, disobedience is a sin and rationalizing over it cost Adam and Eve everything—their Edenic home where divine glory reigned. Losing their Edenic home displaced Adam and Eve from the original home where they were constantly surrounded by the glory of God and thus, they lost their glory—the only normal life they knew. Functioning outside their normal environment created fear, the number one problem plaguing humanity today.

Anytime we find ourselves doing something that is not in accordance with God's will or anytime we find ourselves in a forbidden environment, we will feel discomfort, guilt or shame that causes us to want to run or hide from God and others. Instead we must step out of our hiding places and reach for greater glory. Although in these modern times wrong seems to be right, we cannot allow ourselves to wander away from the paths of righteousness and be lured by the serpent to disobey God's voice as He passes by. Instead we must become agents of greater glory by showing others the way to eternal glory.

Stepping out of one's hiding place calls for reaching—confession and profession. Confessing involves acknowledging one's mistake, asking forgiveness, feeling sorry for injury that was inflicted on another while in a sinful state and restitution—compensating others for what they have lost as a result of their indiscretions. This must be achieved if we are to come to full repentance. One has to repel wrong doings and ingest right doing in order that Christ's grace can be imparted upon him/her, so He can bring back our glory. On the other hand, professing calls for an acknowledgement that one cannot confess in his or her own natural self, human might, but by recognizing that only by God's transforming powers of grace and mercy which enables it.

Even though the price for sins have already been paid, humanity is still struggling with sin as did Adam and Eve. We are still running and hiding to cover the shame of our nakedness—those flaws that the Holy Spirit does not condone. When we disobey our maker, like Adam and Eve, we will wander off into the paths of unrighteousness where recovering glory calls for reaching outside of ourselves. Lurking and wandering away from the paths of righteousness, we become susceptible to the cares of the world: greed, lust, pride, deception and the like which further separate us from the love of God. All of this happens because we live in a world that is not ideally our home. It is why even our associations with family and friends can come between us and God.

Just like Adam and Eve, we are unaware that from the very moment we commit a sinful act we begin to die slowly unless we have conditioned ourselves to recognize such a separation. When and how we deal with severed ties with the Creator varies, but eventually all of us must deal with the separation. Some people die spiritually and emotionally long before dying physically. Thus, they walk around like mummies, dead to the needs of self and others—a shell of their very existence; they are deadened to the empowerment of the Creator. There is no doubt that all of us know the pain of grief and sorrows. Like Adam and Eve, we all have come to know the dreadfulness of sin, but many of us ignore the impact of sin.

Sin negatively affects the relationship between the Creator and His creatures as well as the relationship among His creatures. Additionally, sin affected the relationship between humans and the physical environment. The ground was cursed because of our foreparents' sin. The ground yields not only the beautiful flowers but also the ugly thistles. The impact of sin between humans and the natural environment is further realized after the flood resulting from the immense sin among all people. After the flood, animals became a substitute food supplement; this required animals to relate to humanity in a defensive manner to protect their lives (Genesis 9:2). Isn't it amazing though, that we still have the ability to tame the wild and become one with it, so we can experience a glimpse of the joy, peace and harmony that our first parents once enjoyed more fully.

As it usually happens with humanity, only after losing the glory did Adam and Eve turn to take one last look at all that they had lost and loved. Saddened, they turned to find a strange light gleaming through the darkness in the path they had to take. As they walked towards it, they found that it was a fiery weapon that an angel held in his hand. The light wasn't the glory they may have been anticipating but was aimed at blocking off the path to the tree of life. Adam and Eve realized that there was no going back to the fullness of glory they once knew because the entrance had been blocked off. That was one great price they had to pay for their disobedience. That one little sin surely did cost them and the rest of humanity greatly. While we are lurking in this world that is not ideally ours, we have to go through disappointments, grief and pain that are associated with shattered dreams, and rising above these responses calls for reaching for greater glory.

Chapter 2

SHATTERED HOPES, BROKEN DREAMS

When tragedies strike, we often feel as though we are going through storms and we experience accompanying pain. Such storms can be overwhelmingly chaotic, robbing us of our temporal and eventually ultimate glory. The glory humanity naturally seeks cannot survive adversities. Thus, we experience shattered hopes and broken dreams. Humanity was not designed to live outside of glory and can if we experience what it means to be whole. Imagine how Adam and Eve felt after they lost glory as they found themselves in an unusually corrupt environment that was quite different from anything they had known.

The fact that we suffer shattered hopes and broken dream is a clear indication that we are investing in the wrong kingdom. God sent His Son to bring a part of His Kingdom down to earth so that we may have hope of returning to greater glory. Christ has taught us how to pray that God's Kingdom comes on earth as it is in Heaven' (Matthew 5) but instead of reaching for greater glory, beyond the momentary thrill of instant gratification, we improvise by building or investing in earthly empires. These earthly kingdoms are designed to make up for what was lost but to no avail, for in this world kingdoms may rise and will surely fall. Only God's Kingdom stands forever. If we place our treasures in earthly kingdoms, we may be gratified temporarily but when they fall, so will our hopes and dreams.

While humanity is weak and vulnerable to the pains that taunt us, each of us varies in the way we respond to painful situations. Oftentimes the way we respond to painful situations may cause us more pain than the adversity that initially disrupted our lives. If we respond and reach out as Esther, Daniel, and Job did in their time of turmoil, we would receive the victory and greater glory. Each of these persons had three common characteristics: 1) lived a lifestyle based on godly principles not just religious behavior; 2) allowed their comfort zone of existence to become shaken without losing faith; 3) willingly faced death knowing there was hope beyond. All three persons looked beyond their immediate painful circumstance to the horizon. Unlike these three God-conscious individuals, many of us tend to revert to behaviors that subject us to more injury than we experience while going through the storms and the pain. According to Antoine de Saint Exupery, "The meaning of things lies not in the things themselves, but in our attitude towards them."

Negative behaviors, thoughts and attitudes can impact our prospect of finding hope, joy and peace within as well as destroy harmony with others and our Creator. Such behaviors defer our dreams causing us to ask the questions raised in Langston Hughes[1],

"Harlem" regarding deferred dreams: "Does it dry up like a raisin in the sun? Or fester like a sore/and then run? Or does it explode?" While there may be any number of causes for dreams to become shattered, I have found that it's how we handle our shattered dreams that determines how quickly we rebound from them. Our thoughts control our actions; our actions determine our habits, which form our character that gives birth to our destiny. Guarding our thoughts helps us fit the broken empty pieces back together again or discard them altogether, if necessary.

Many of us take the time out to plan for successful dreams, but planning cannot guarantee that things will go as we have planned. Oftentimes, when things do not go as planned they tend to injure and disparage us but:

> *Just because the solutions of problems are not visible at any particular time does not mean that those problems will never be alleviated— or confined to tolerable dimensions. History has a way of changing the very terms in which problems operate and of leaving them, in the end, unsolved, to be sure, yet strangely deflated of their original meaning and importance"* (Abramowitz).

Many of us don't create contingency plans because we don't anticipate mishaps and, according to Orison S. Marsden, *"Our destiny changes with our thought; we shall become what we wish to become, do what we wish to do, when our habitual thought corresponds with our desire."* There are some that map out everything, but no matter how well one plans out life, things will not always play out as planned.

We must realize that we do not live unto ourselves; there are some things we cannot plan for because they are not within our control. However, our response to these unexpected situations is within our sphere of control. Life runs its own course on a planet where gravity always wins, "for what goes up must come back down." Therefore, it would be wise to exhibit caution in all planned affairs, for there will always be circumstances and people who interfere with our plans trying to wreak havoc, which can shatter our hopes and dreams. What is one to do once her hopes are shattered and dreams are broken?

Prior to September 11, 2001, many Americans, regular people like myself, had big plans and glorious dreams for a bright future. Even though the economy was already showing signs of spiraling downwards like a descending roller coaster, most of us thought that with education, finances and job stability we could quickly steer our lives back on course. Given all the economic shifts since 9-11, even upper class families are now complaining that they feel a little unsure about their financial future. Companies within the travel industry have taken major hits that forced them to cutback; some of them have even applied for government assistance to bail them out. Although the economy seems to be picking back up, with news about Enron and Microsoft rocked the stock markets back and forth, both big and small businesses have folded. Gas prices seem to soar higher with threats regarding the Middle East and its impact on the rest of the world.

During the 2001 Christmas season, I was listening to a local radio station. One man called in to request a song that he said brought cheer to him because he was feeling like his job security was enormously threatened. It was the fourth time within the last few months he was forced to transfer to another city to keep his job. Also, a manager for Delta Airlines was obviously concerned about the layoffs from top level management on down; he was seen on the evening news shortly after September 11 saying that he was willing to work without pay for six months to keep his job. Usually it is the small business that seems to become most affected by tragedies like this; however, many large businesses including some Fortune 500 hundred companies have lost assets, business, equity and security. They have been forced to cut back in places experts couldn't forecast. Some of these areas were never faced as pressing issues in their strategic planning sessions; thus, they have been faced with great and unexpected catastrophes.

The question that was on the minds of many Americans after hearing some of the financial quotas was not if they are on the list but when would they get their pink slip. People have lost what they perceived to have been glory; even in the aftermath when the economy seems to be picking up, many are still afraid to board their flights, afraid to open their mail and afraid about their financial future. Prior to that now dreaded September day, many who had good jobs, financial security and bright prospects were looking for ways to increase their company's capital, so they could gain the competitive advantage among their colleagues. Others were planning ways to climb up the corporate ladder of success. Some were even playing the old work game by plotting to flatten the tires of others trying to stop them from moving further ahead or anticipating stepping on another's toe to get ahead. For some, before September11 became a fateful day, the week was the beginning of their bright future in a career with opportunities to grow and develop. Unfortunately, life does not always unravel the way we plan it, and many who invested solely in this earthly empire were in for a rude awakening when the resources in which they invested crumbled as a result of the events.

Up until the morning of September 11, many of us were busy trying to fulfill our own dreams in life, and many of us thought we were living gloriously, but we surrendered as life dealt us a deadly blow. Like Nathaniel Hawthorne's Young Goodman Brown in "Young Goodman Brown," the protagonist asked in his crisis in the woods, *"But where is Faith?"* Moments before, he cried, *"my Faith is gone!"* The last thing we hear Young Goodman Brown cry is *"Faith, Faith...look up to heaven, and resist the wicked one."* What he should have asked was *"What kind of faith do I possess?" "Where is my faith?" "Is my faith in myself, others, things or in the God of heaven's faithfulness?"*[2] Young Goodman Brown's final experience was one of dismal disappointment without hope. Most of us have been like or are like Young Goodman Brown; we do not rely solely on the LORD's faithfulness; we do not see the big picture beyond present circumstances. Many of us cannot get beyond the temporal grave to the eternal glory. The self-centered and self-serving glory we have is insufficient in times of shattered dreams, but the glory obtained from God remains constant amid the changing misfortunes in life. However, as Thomas Jefferson best puts it, *"Nothing can stop the (individual) with the right mental attitude from achieving his goal; nothing on earth can help the (individual) with the wrong mental attitude."*

In the aftermath of the sinister attacks, terrorism continues to plague us in the form of biological attacks, anthrax, and further threats on American soil. Even though America is fighting back and appears to be winning the war against terrorism, it is difficult for those who had family and friends trapped in the walls of those crumbling building to move ahead with their lives in a normal fashion. Getting back to normal is a slogan of great pain; what people need is the time and tools to face the tragedy, trace the tragedy, accept the tragedy, and erase (i.e., move beyond) the tragedy. Some people are still haunted by nightmares from the damaging images they saw flashing across their television screens—Post-Traumatic Stress Syndrome is what psychologists call it.

Many experts have been bombarded with questions about how people at different ages should respond to the changes in the aftermath. A Child Psychologist of New York University, Robin Goodman, told an Iyanla talk show audience that a young child would think the catastrophic events are still happening if it keeps playing over and over again on the television screen. She believes that children respond differently based upon how they receive the information and how their parents handle the information. Here is a synopsis of how Goodman views people at different age ranges respond to post-traumatic stress.

Age Range	How A Typical Child Reacts To Crisis	How an Adult/Parent Should Respond To A Child's Reactions
0-4	• Cries a lot and gets irritated • Problem sleeping and eating • Gets clingy: holds tight	• Reassures the child • Holds the child
5-12	• Expresses Anger • Regresses • Withdrawals	• Engages child in positive and fun activities, so s/he can feel in control • Sets limits for the child • Does fun activities with child
13-19	• Gets angry and depressed • Becomes hopeless • Will have long term effect	• Treats child like an adult • Models the desired behavior • Opens dialogue

Since September 11, 2001, the people of America have found themselves in a similar situation to Adam and Eve when they first became displaced from the mainstream of what they had known life to be; a new normalcy has formed. Like any traumatic experience, our sense of normalcy shifts, but it can shift without blocking access to temporal glory—joy, hope, peace and harmony. Coping with uncertainties that we face in the aftermath of 9-11 is possible when we are reaching for greater glory in a quest to find our way back home.

Peace is not the absence of turmoil but the ability to maintain balance in the midst of the turmoil. Surely, the work of Satan is to prevent people from recovering from a loss of temporal glory; thus, diminishing the prospect of seeing the ultimate glory. This he does to keep us focused on our shattered hopes and broken dreams rather than on the desire of moving beyond them to reach for greater glory.

I would never forget that morning when my husband called my attention to the attack as it unfolded live on television. So overwhelmed, I stopped to pray for those in the buildings and planes. I also prayed for those loved ones that witnessed such an awful atrocity. Among all the things I had heard and seen, there was no doubt in my mind that this was the worst tragedy in America's history. I rose in shock to the burning towers then watched people jumping out of windows that were dozens of stories high. As the reality of the crumbling buildings set in, I caved in with dismay. I became so numb and felt so helpless that the only thing I could think of was "prayer"! My initial response was to keep on praying for the safety of the innocent bystanders and that those who committed such a horrendous crime against humanity would be found and brought to justice. I felt nauseous, reacting emotionally as I thought of the hundreds of families that were ravaged by this terrible act, not only in New York but all across the nation and around the world. I stayed glued to my television until I became overwhelmed. I then realized what I could do to help hurting people to get through the storm and the pain and get back the temporal glory many lost that day and previously.

I know one person who had lost a loved one in the attacks, if it affected me so profusely, I can't imagine how those directly affected by it really felt. Those of us reaching for greater glory understand the plight of others and are touched by the feelings of their infirmities, for we know that as we try to function in a world that was not exclusively ours we must pay the penalty along with the rest of humanity.

You, too, may be dismayed about the sinister attack and feel disdain directed towards America. Although America has been fighting back with retaliatory strikes and seems to be winning the war against terrorism, many are still afraid of the unknown because people are aware that it can neither strengthen the economy, give children back their lost innocence nor stop the dreadful feeling. People are still so angry, fearful, hateful, guilt-ridden and sorrowful that they need more than a war to bring back their glory. Until people find a sweet relief, the travel industry will continue to have problems getting the masses to trust in them, the government is going to have a difficult time encouraging people to put faith in them, and parents are going to have a difficult time consoling and controlling children.

Usually when national trouble strikes, our politicians, police agencies, spiritual leaders, parents, legal counsel, and educational personnel can easily help us get our lives together again. However, there are crises like September 11 when everyone is looking for solutions, but there are no immediate answers. As time goes by, people are feeling a little release but no real glory. While the answers are evident, many of us are so out of touch with reality that we don't want to see the obvious, so we turn to other means which only intensify our problems. Only an optimist can see opportunity while going through adversity. Said Sir Winston Churchill in one of his famous speeches, *"A pessimist sees the difficulty in every opportunity, an optimist sees the opportunity in every difficulty."* Instead of seeing the opportunity in this difficult time and turning to God from where our relief comes, some of us see the difficulty in every opportunity and have turned to drugs, alcohol, friends and cosmic powers for answers. However, no amount of psychics, palm readers, witchcraft, zodiac or voodoo can bring our temporal glory back. We have lost our glory, and the only way to gain it back is to turn back to the source of our light and power. By reaching, we can find the joy, peace and comfort that we need in difficult times, for they are not easily accessible without the originator. Glory is a gift from God. If we continue to turn away from the path of righteousness, we will only dig a ditch deeper than we can climb out of. To get the assurance we need to find comfort, joy and peace—when we are in harmony with the creator—we must tap into God amid the turbulent storm and the eye of pain that shatters our hopes and dreams.

In the aftermath of tragic events like September 11, it is time that we let go of our selfish desires and reach for the glory. Many of us seem to have been mesmerized by the appearance of calm as we drift past the trauma of September 11 but according to Fredrick A. Russell, Pastor of Miracle Temple SDA Church, *"Calm is deceptive."* The reason Russell gives for this is that, *"Determined people of evil intent can and will probe our country's weaknesses for future attacks."* We must stop focusing on our shattered *hopes and broken dreams and look to the plan that God has for our individual lives for according to Russell, "The threats, dangers, anxiety, pressures, and stresses of this life will never go away down here. They will only cease when we get to our "real home."*[3] Despite continued adversities that Satan puts around us, if we can see the plots of the enemy as merely detours rather than roadblocks along the road to glory and reach for greater glory then we can get a foretaste of God's glory. This foretaste will lead us to live liberated and fulfilling lives. That glimpse can give us a vision that will carry us through this earth until we reach our final destiny, eternity, *for "it only takes a spark to get a fire going!"* Of course, Satan is going to continually keep trying to dim that spark because he knows that once it is ignited, we will have the power to resist him. The only way to reach for greater glory is to keep our eyes fixed on the Savior. This fixation calls for striking a balance between our personal relationship with God and living a meaningful life on this earth despite our obstacles.

If we allow our own personal goals and dreams to take a backseat to God, we ought not to become surprised when Satan attempts to lure us away much like he did with Eve and Adam. Satan doesn't want us to have our temporal glory nor have the prospect of ultimate glory while on his territory. That's why the Bible admonishes us to "be sober, be vigilant;" for God knows that our *"adversary the devil, as a roaring lion, walketh about, seeking whom he can devour"* (1 Peter 5:3).

All the tragedies, adversities and evils in the world today are making it increasingly more difficult for us to become reconciled back to God to receive His full glory.

When we begin to wander from God, Satan makes it absolutely difficult for us to get back on track. He will use, greed, other people, material possessions, past short comings, present ignorance, utter arrogance and any other human frailty to keep us trapped in darkness and blinded to the light of God's glory that is right in our midst.

Sin and evil seem enticing, initially, but they rob us of our joy, peace, comfort and salvation—eventually! Once we begin to play around with sin, cultivate evil thoughts, carry out wicked acts or get caught up with worldly possessions, little by little we will strangle the connection that we have with God. Despite the fact that the Holy Spirit still pleads with us in our innermost being, our sanctuary where the LORD longs to reside, all those things we get caught up with become like noise, blocking out or interrupting any possibility of hearing God's plea. Some things we get caught up with can be used for Satan's advantage, if we are not careful, we can collect demons. Once these demons find a breathing place in our inner being, only God in love and mercy can remove them.

The worldly things we get caught up with as we coexist in our earthly empire become baggage, which weigh us down to block God's glory from being revealed in our lives. We may be satisfied; however, we will not have the courage to stand up for what is right when adversity comes unless we allow God's glory to shine in our lives. Much of our darkened circumstances, which lead to devastating results, stems from excess baggage. It is much like the dreaded event involving R & B star Aliyah. As evidence now has shown, this young and talented female who had nothing but stardom on the horizon despite warnings, insisted on flying from the Bahamas with all the excesses she had acquired. All that she had was too much for the plane that functioned as normal. The weight of all the baggage prevented the plane from performing its normal expected duty and instead of smoothly soaring upwards, the excess weight propelled it downwards. Death and severance of ties could have been avoided had all the unnecessary baggage been dumped. Although she has received many awards since her death, she is unable to enjoy all the accolades. Oh, how tragic baggage can become in our physical as well as spiritual, mental and social lives. Now is the perfect time to familiarize ourselves with God's plan so that when adversity comes we will neither lose sight of God's glory nor feel the sting of guilt that sin has left on us.

We can make it through storms and pain only as we develop a hope beyond and reach farther than the sentimental things we possess today. Until the God of creation brings us back into His Glory, life may never get back to normal as we once knew it. However, we can make it better if we rise above our past and present circumstances no matter how grim things may appear. Going back to normal may, in fact, be the worst thing to desire given where it has led us. However, we do not have to walk around life mad at the world, blaming others for our mishaps or feeling fearful, sorrowful or hurtful any longer than is necessary if we are headed home. There is hope for tomorrow, but it depends on whom or in what we put our trust. It is all well that America is fighting back to try to regain some control of the problems we are experiencing at home; however, it would be nice if they that could have brought back the glory we lost September 11, but that is impossible. In this world, empires may rise and they will also fall, but if we put our trust in our Creator and invest in His eternity we will never have need to worry even though circumstances are constantly changing around us. Balance can only be experienced when we are not dis-eased with being fully human and alive in the presence of the LORD and fellow human beings. There is only one thing that can give us the peace we need when our dreams are shattered, refuge in God's glory. That is why it is necessary to reach for greater glory while it is rightfully ours. By reaching out, we will get the blessing and rewards.

Thus, it is necessary for humanity to reach for greater glory which is attainable if one is willing to tap into a higher source of power which is not hard since God has put a plan of salvation in place to reconcile us back to Him. Right within our hearts, our Heavenly Father has planted a Spirit to guide us into all truth. If we learn to tap into that source then we can attain greater glory, not just temporarily but ultimately, for God has provided signs down through the ages to help us find our way back to Eden—our lost home. To regain our lost glory we have to let go of self, so we can see and understand what those signs represent and let God point us in the right direction.

Chapter 3

SIGNS AND WONDERS OF OUR TIMES

God is moving by His spirit all over this world today; those who are not seeing His signs and wonders in these days may not be positioning themselves to reach for greater glory. As God moves, He is pouring out His Holy Spirit on brave men and women (Acts 2:17, 18) much like He did with the apostles of Christ. Though the LORD refused to specify times or seasons to His disciples, He warned them of the unveiling power of the Holy Ghost that would come upon them, turning them into witnesses (Acts 2:7, 8). Those who can't see the light of God's glory may have gotten so caught up in the affairs of this earth that it is causing them to miss out on the joys of being in harmony with Him. Though some may not believe it, I agree with Hannah Whitall Smith's article, Is God in Everything? Cited on the Internet shortly after the attacks on September 11, 2001:

No person or company of people, no power in earth or heaven, can touch that soul which is abiding in Christ, without first passing through His encircling presence, and receiving the seal of His permission. If God be for us, it matters not who may be against us; nothing can disturb or harm us, except He shall see that it is best for us, and shall stand aside to let it pass. An earthly parent's care for his helpless child is a feeble illustration of this. If the child is in its father's arms, nothing can touch it without that father's consent, unless he is too weak to prevent it. And even if this should be the case, he suffers the harm first in his own person before he allows it to reach his child. If an earthly parent would thus care for his little helpless one, how much more will our heavenly Father, whose love is infinitely greater, and whose strength and wisdom can never be baffled, care for us! What is needed, then, is to see God in everything, and to receive everything directly from His hands, with no intervention of second causes; and it is to just this that we must be brought before we can know an abiding experience of entire abandonment and PERFECT TRUST. Our abandonment must be to God, not to man; and our TRUST MUST BE IN HIM, not in any arm of flesh, or we shall fail at the first trial (Nahum 1:7, Deuteronomy 33:27, Psalm 9:10, and 32:10).

The signs and wonders we see around us are indications of God's moving in human affairs, and we have no need to fear with God at hand to bless. Signs are like beams of light beckoning us that God is about to finish His work. He wants to remind us of our duty and the promises He made to Eve that her seed shall bruise the head of the serpent. As God moves, He is looking for strong men and women who are able to stand up for what is right and reach for greater glory so that He can empower us to fulfill His promises. As He passes by,

He mends our lives along the way by both waking us up when we slumber in defeat and touching us while groping in darkness. Unaware that God is touching people to raise up a standard in this generation, many of us stand in disbelief of why God wants to use us, but He has awakened us to live in full surrender to Him. He calls people to serve Him and place them under His arrest by the empowering of the Holy Spirit. It's time to take a good look at ourselves and our world to notice that something significant is going to come out of all the chaos and revelation around us. After the storms of life comes the sunshine, the glory, for those who are positioned to bask in it. A song I vaguely recall to memory says, *"behind every dark cloud, there is a silver lining."* To position oneself to receive greater glory, one has to look at signs and wonders as well as endure hardship.

The disorder we see in the world around us today are signs of the time that we are living in. Recently, we have seen the tyranny of terrorism take its toll on American soil. Many casualties, deaths and ongoing biological scare tactics have changed the way we live in reality. The unrest we see around us is not just mere coincidence; it's an indication of the sign that God is setting the scene for the ultimate great controversy— the final conflict that will transpire between Satan and Him. Our part in the conflict is to bruise the heel of the snake, Satan, who has orchestrated all of this evil. This originator of our stolen glory will be brought to judgment but in the meantime, He wants to reap havoc on God's children. While Satan is gathering his army against God's people, God does not want us to be unaware of what is about to transpire, so He hands down hints throughout history as far back as the writings of Daniel and the writings of John the Revelator. He did not leave His work unfinished with the apostle Paul because He has and is still using men and women to prepare His people for what is going to happen soon.

When I was a little girl, I often heard "Jesus is coming soon." I took it seriously, though sometimes I had my doubts and questions. Constantly searching for truths prepared me for end time events now taking place in the world around me. All the preparation helped me to recognize that the things that are happening around me are signs that are relevant to end time events. The song "Redemption Draweth Nigh" by Gordon Jenson still remains one of my favorites and is quite fitting for these present troubling times.

Years of time have come and gone
Since I first heard it told,
How Jesus would come again someday;
If back then it seems so real,
Then I just can't help but feel
How much closer His coming is today.

Wars and strife on every hand,
And violence fills our land,
Still some people doubt He'll come again;
But the word of God is true,
He'll redeem His chosen few
Don't loose hope, soon Christ Jesus will descend.

Signs of the times are everywhere,
And there's a brand new feeling in the air,
Keep your eyes upon the eastern skies;
Lift up your head redemption draweth nigh.

Essentials of the Time Factor

Time is a significant factor that impacts the way we perceive signs and wonders in the world today, and we can't get our temporal glory back unless we are fully aware of the importance of time in our lives. Our perception of time can influence how we see the significance in the things that are taking place in the world around us. Many of us see time as the here and now—carpe diem (seize ye the day), but time could have never existed if history didn't repeat itself. Similarly, history keeps repeating itself as humanity keeps making the same mistakes of Adam and Eve. How we view time is based on our limited perceptions of reality, but people who dedicate their lives to the study of historical time tend to measure it based on comparing trends from past events with present-day circumstances. When looking at time, we may take it for granted, figuring that it is ours for the keeping.

Regardless of how time is measured, it dictates our standard of living and our thought processes. Time is often viewed in temporal terms for we tend to view history as only the here and now. Time plays more of a significant role in our lives than we are aware. It is difficult for us to make headway if we can't trace our past because it is our past that helps us to find our rich heritage that shapes the standard of living in our present world; thus, giving us hope that carries us through the uncertainties of tomorrow. The past is the source of what was right and what went wrong; it is the source of the problem and the solution.

When we are faced with the unknown past or present, we are apt to become resistant and tend to disassociate ourselves from the problem, taking no ownership for potential negative behaviors or actions. We see problems as not ideally ours but as someone else's. Rather than trying to adapt or change we become more reluctant and thus rob ourselves of future glory. The longer we go with such a mentality, the more miserable we become because when the ball is in another's court, we tend to lose control.

Even though we live in a modern world that is constantly challenged by uncertainties, we come face to face with things we can't fathom and are quick to protest, riot or make demands rather than trying to become more adaptive. We live in a society that is driven by change and diversity, yet we still idealize familiarity. Most of us do not have the strength or the courage to face uncertainties and difficulties gracefully because we do not position ourselves to receive greater glory. The numerous and diverse changes that are made in this modern society contributes to us developing feelings of insecurities. For instance, some of us become so stressed when we are surrounded by people of a different race, sex, culture or background that we tend to lose our ability to reason rationally. We believe that time is on our side and put off ways to relieve our stress, especially when it calls for searching our past experiences, the origin of our stress.

We tend to take time for granted thinking it will always be at our disposal without interruption, and we can control it although there will come a time when all of us will have to give an account of how we have spent our time here on earth. Everyone has a concept of life after death. However, the reality remains that after death then comes the judgment or the full glory from the Creator. At this point in time, we can only reach for greater glory, which is temporal in nature. While living in this world we have to put time into perspective, see the signs and wonders that are beckoning us to receive full glory and continually position ourselves to have a chance of attaining it.

God is planning a time to bring an end to all the confusion in this world. The signs and wonders around us are ushering in this grand finale. Instead of getting sidetracked by all the signs and wonders around us, worried about when or where another terrorist will strike, when the next bio/chemical attack will be launched or if countries like South Korea will use its chemical weaponry, we should be more concerned about what these troubling times represent. Yet, what we don't seem to be concerned with at all, is how we can get back our temporal glory during the time we have left on this earth. What we ought to concern ourselves with is not what is going to happen to us, not when or if, but <u>when</u> God is going to show up. He is the only one that can put a real damper on time for humanity. Unless we are positioning ourselves to live gloriously, carrying the good news of Salvation to all we meet as Christ taught in times past, we cannot be one with God when He comes. Only those who are faithful will refuse to allow fear to ruin their lives, for they know that God is a being far greater than any biological weaponry or chemical bombs. All who plan to survive need to begin reaching out for greater glory now.

End Time Issues

Since the fall of Satan, humanity has been groping around in darkness, but God wants to show us His full glory, one that has not been seen even by Adam and Eve. God can bring back temporary glory in this earth to make us truly happy and at peace amid the ills around us, but He can only do it on an individual basis since we are in the environment of sin. However, no earthly glory can be compared to the awe of God's presence towards which He points us through end time signs.

Americans have put up with individual crimes, which occasionally are crimes of passion, but no American was prepared for the senseless terrorist attacks that struck the homeland in such a split second. Amid all of the terror, we are encouraged to lift up our heads when we see these signs for our redemption draws near. Fulfilled prophecies indicate that we are beginning to see the end of times. If we look around, it is evident that something more catastrophic than what is transpiring in the world around us will take place soon. Aside from the wars and rumors of wars we see taking place around us, signs like "*global warming*" (Revelations 16:8,9), *Nations are becoming angrier with other nations* (Matthew 24:7; Revelations 11:18), *chaos and confusion in the world* (Luke 21:25), and a *world that is divided over faith* (Revelations 13:9-12). Nature also reveals some *unusual events that are taking place in the sky* (Matthew 24:29) that according to Robert Frost, American poet, *"How many times it thundered before Franklin took the hint! How many apples fell on*

Newton's head before he took the hint! Nature is always hinting at us. And suddenly we take the hint." We also see *unpredictable earthquakes, unexpected storms* and *natural disasters* becoming more prevalent and severe (Luke 21:26; Revelations 6:12-15; 16:19-21; Mark 13:19-23; 1 Thessalonians 2:8-12). There is an overwhelming *desire for demonic intervention* and an *acceptance and spread of modern spiritualism* (1 Timothy 4:1). Recently, we see increased social unrest, *economic troubles* (James. 5:1-6), *knowledge increase* (Daniel 12:4) and *apostasy: contempt for faith* (2 Timothy 3:1-5) as God's people suffer immensely from persecution (Revelations 13:15-17). All of these signs point us to God's soon return to reveal His ultimate glory and redeem His chosen few.

Despite the things that transpire during the end of time, God does not want us to live in fear or become complacent because the end is not yet. Christ promised that all those aforementioned things must come to pass before His return, but He wants us to continue the work He has begun in us. Jesus did not give signs to overwhelm us or force us into speculation about the end but to remind us of His teaching, where He encouraged four things: *watchfulness, endurance* to the end, *preaching/teaching* the word and *be not deceived*. Christ ascribed rewards to those who position themselves for greater glory by being obedient to Him. He said, *"He that endures unto the end, the same shall be saved"* and *"this gospel of the kingdom shall be preached in all the world for a witness unto all nations; and then shall the end come"*(Matthew 24:13,14). Though signs are unfolding around us, the end is not yet for the work of God must be fulfilled in the earth first.

Amid all the confusion and misinterpretation of end time issues, signs are meant to motivate and warn us to finish the work on earth. We won't see eternal glory until the message of Salvation through Christ for a dying people in a dark world has reached the utmost parts of the world. When we see the signs of the end times, we must ask God to help us find our place and show us His glory as the earth becomes darkened by Satan's deceptions. Repeatedly, we must intercede with God on each other's behalf and position ourselves to reach for greater glory, then allow God to give us temporal glory amid the difficulties we face each day.

A Recent Prophecy That Was Fulfilled

Many Bible scholars believe that the United States of America has a significant presence in prophecy and end time events but not many know exactly how it will play out. The things happening in America are no surprise to well-studied spiritually minded people. For years, Bible scholars have followed the doctrines of what one may call a modern day prophetess, Ellen G. White. Over the years, her work has impacted some of the most prestigious editorials, like *Time Magazine*. Many have found her account of prophetic events pretty accurate, but as with everything else, there are skeptics who try to undermine her revelations. Whether one believes or not is up to his conscience and convictions, but the following excerpt is one of her predictions that was highly publicized after the events that transpired in New York City on September 11, 2001.

God has not executed His wrath without mercy. His hand is stretched out still. His message must be given in Greater New York. The people must be shown how it is possible for God, by a touch of His hand, to destroy the property they have gathered together against the last great day. ~3MR 310, 311 (1902).

I have no light in particular in regard to what is coming on New York, only that I know that one day the great building there will be thrown down by the turning and overturning of God's power... Death will come in all places. This is why I am so anxious for our cities to be warned. ~Review and Herald July 5, 1906.

*Feb. 15, 1904: On one occasion, when in **New York City**, I was in the night season called upon to behold buildings rising story after story toward heaven. These buildings were warranted to be fireproof, and they were erected to glorify their owners and builders... Higher and still higher these buildings rose, and in them the most costly material was used... {Life Sketches of Ellen G. White 413.2} "As these lofty buildings went up, the owners rejoiced with ambitious pride that they had money to use in glorifying self... Much of the money that they thus invested had been obtained through exaction, through grinding the faces of the poor. In the books of heaven, an account of every business transaction is kept. There every unjust deal, every fraudulent act, is recorded. The time is coming when in their*

> *fraud and insolence men will reach a point that the Lord will not permit them to pass, and they will learn that there is a limit to the forbearance of Jehovah. {Ibid 413.3}*
>
> *The scene that next passed before me was an alarm of fire. Men looked at the loft and supposedly fireproof buildings and said: "They are perfectly safe." But these buildings were consumed as if made of pitch. The fire engines could do nothing to stay the destruction. The firemen were unable to operate the engines. Testimonies Vol. 9" 12,13 (1909).*
>
>

"LAST DAY EVENTS" by Ellen G. White (Pg. 112-113)
>

Keep in mind that the foresight of signs to come were not only revealed through prophets of old but also people of today. This forecast of signs to come signifies that signs of the end times are not only revealed through prophets and messiahs but through ordinary people, like you and me, in the form of prophecy. Joel 2:28 envisioned a day like September11 would come when God will pour out His Spirit to empower us to dream and prophesy.

Present Day Facts Which Relate To End Time Signs

Since the events that took place on September 11, 2001, Americans no longer have that invincible feeling they once had. The impregnable illusion has been broken, filling man's hearts with fear and arousing everyone's awareness to the forces of evil all around. We are in a time when biblical prophecies are coming true as many hearts are failing for fear. The events that accompanied the September 11 tragedy caused the young and rising generation to lose its innocence, complacency in its comfort zone. That day started out as people performed their daily routine: sipping coffee, sending emails, attending meetings, and the next moment they were overcome by shattering windows, burning buildings, and crumbling walls. For one moment, everything seemed normal but as the events unfolded, people desperately ran in terror and fear to get out of harm's way. Even those at the highest level of our hierarchy ran for cover that day.

Humanly, everyone in the vicinity ran for his or her safety for a brief moment until they came to the realization that people were hurting and dying. That's when the humanitarian evolved in those that stopped to do good by lending a helping hand wherever and however they could. Since this tragedy, most Americans no longer take life for granted. Even in the aftermath, it doesn't appear that America will ever be the same again. While people are going back to their daily routine, they don't feel any less lost, confused or fearful than that day. Some are learning how to pick up the broken and empty pieces, but like people in earlier times we must all accept that a new norm has been set. The new norm includes a spiritual awakening for many people and alertness for others.

The True Purpose of Prophecy

To fight the spiritual warfare and win, we must understand the true purpose of prophecy so that we can be clothed in God's glory which will sustain us when the battle intensifies. It's imperative not to disregard

God's purpose for providing prophecy. Understanding the true purpose of prophecy helps us realize the signs of the times that we live in and makes us want to share this light with all who are willing to listen and obey. It takes an honest and open heart that is receptive to change to grasp the concept of the true purpose of prophecy.

Signs around us suggest that we are nearing our final destiny—a return to our full glory; this is not a dooms-day message but a glorious welcome. Jesus revealed that prophecies are foretold so that when they come to pass, we will believe in Him (John 13:19). When signs are unveiled around us, we must not speculate or make any predictions of Christ's return. They are only to remind us of the words that Jesus spoke that encourages us to be *watchful*, *endure hardship*, *repent*, *witness*, *be sober* and *vigilant*. Recently some signs have been fulfilled right before our very eyes, but to most people these signs do not seem odd. Only those who are spiritually connected to God understand the teachings of Christ and can relate the significance to modern day signs.

Years ago I read a devotional book that specified two types of destructive attitudes that most of us tend to develop in regards to life: over-reacting and under-reacting. It suggested that most people either over react or under react to situations. Interestingly enough, I find that people around me tend to under-react to the conditions that are tearing down our community and the world around us via abuse, crime, drugs, homelessness, sexual exploitation and trickery, but they overreact to the worldly allurements such as fashion, finances and material possessions. Our response to the signs and wonders are no different and both over-reacting and under-reacting can have a profound impact on our reach for glory. Here's an up-close look at the flip side of both attitudes.

- **Over-reactors** are described as those people that usually become alarmed easily about events that are taking place around them. Oftentimes, they may assign suggestive significance to every war or catastrophe that transpires. This group may cause others to go into false excitement that tends to lead to a lack of concern when events don't follow their expectations. They are like the man who kept crying "wolf, wolf," but no wolf came. Then one day the wolf came, but no one came to his defense. Over reacting to the little things in life and signs of the times may eventually lead to feelings of disappointment or disbelief and may cause no one to become alarmed when there is a real need for concern.

- **Under-reactors** are depicted as those people that usually refuse to recognize the urgency of situations in life. For example, people who fail to see the vital signs and events that foretell the nearness of Christ's return. People who under-react usually tend to be unresponsive to things that cause spiritual awakening. They are often unaware of things in plain view that are worth seeing. This kind of attitude often leads to complacency and separation from the presence of others and the Holy Spirit. The people in the day of Noah that refused to adhere to the warnings and refused to obey until the storms began serve as another example of people under-reacting. Despite signs and wonders that signify the times we live in, many still under-react and don't feel the need to reach for greater glory. Thus, they deprive themselves of the temporal glory that may lead to a loss of eternal glory.

There is a profound state of complacency among people including Christians. Many people in our generation take lightly the significance regarding end time issues. Even though the end may not be yet (1Thessalonians 5: 4-7), warns against being ignorant about the signs of the times we live in. Ignorance can cause us to lose both temporal and eternal glory. When prophecies are being fulfilled, we must wake up from our slumber, believe in Christ (John 13:19), be watchful and ready. Complacency is prevalent not only to generation X and Y but also among the baby boomers and seniors. Many of us live our lives just for today. That may be all well and good, but what happens if there is no tomorrow, and we have to account for all our actions of today?

If Tomorrow Never Comes

If I knew it would be the last time
that I'd see you fall asleep,
I would tuck you in more tightly
and pray the Lord, your soul to keep.

If I knew it would be the last time
that I see you walk out the door,
I would give you a hug and kiss
and call you back for one more.

If I knew it would be the last time
I'd hear your voice lifted up in praise,
I would video tape each action and word,
so I could play them back day after day.

If I knew it would be the last time,
I could spare an extra minute or two
to stop and say I love you,
instead of assuming you would KNOW I do.

If I knew it would be the last time
I would be there to share your day,
well I'm sure you'll have so many more,
so I can let just this one slip away.

For surely there's always tomorrow
to make up for an oversight,
and we always get a second chance
to make everything right.

There will always be another day
to say our "I love you's,"
And certainly there's another chance
to say our "Anything I can do's?"

But just in case I might be wrong,
and today is all I get,
I'd like to say how much I love you
and I hope we never forget,

Tomorrow is not promised to anyone,
young or old alike,
And today may be the last chance you get
to hold your loved one tight.

So if you're waiting for tomorrow,
why not do it today?
For if tomorrow never comes,
you'll surely regret the day,

That you didn't take that extra time
for a smile, a hug, or a kiss
and you were too busy to grant someone,
what turned out to be their one last wish.

So hold your loved ones close today,
whisper in their ear,
Tell them how much you love them
and that you'll always hold them dear,

Take time to say "I'm sorry, please forgive me,"
"thank you" or "it's okay".
And if tomorrow never comes,
you'll have no regrets about today.
Author Unknown

Striking a balance in our lives is a wise choice because humanity has both the mental aptitudes to both live productively today and live in expectancy that the world may end any time. Christ may not come tomorrow, but life is not guaranteed either; in the final analysis, the only thing that really matters is our spiritual connection to God. It is time that we get closer to God and finish the work that He has began in us instead of moping around in life, trivializing over things we have little or no control over. Being amazed about the truths, the facts that are revealed or obsessed with signs and wonders are not enough to merit us any favor with God. Time has a way of slipping by. As those precious moments come and go, if we aren't in oneness with God, He cannot build a hedge of protection enabling us to stand in the tougher times, which are ahead.

Signs and wonders are only to remind us to reach for greater glory by putting our faith into action as we are going out to spread the good news of salvation. Our true focus should be finding personal salvation and letting our lights shine in this dark world so grimaced by threats and uncertainty. Our human duty is to let God's beauty be seen in us. If someone asks, "Where is your faith amid all of this dread?" What will your answer be? Don't be fooled, if we are not aware and prepared, not knowing what to expect in tough times, we can be easily deceived. God expects the best from us. When we follow after righteousness, God can bring us into realms where we can live gloriously even in adverse times. When we do, Christ's beauty can be seen in us. God has promised to bring back temporal glory into our lives so that we're comforted, retain our joy, find peace within and live in harmony in the midst of the storm.

Bad things may happen, but we can be prepared for disappointments and mishaps, which may cause us to doubt, give up hope or loose faith. Signs around us are revealing and must be taken seriously because they can point us to ultimate Glory. Troublesome signs should not discourage us because they have been foretold; they should cause to draw nearer to the Creator.

Chapter 4

WHY TROUBLES PLAGUE US

Troubles have their cause; they plague us when we or others around us are not rightly positioned to embrace God's glory, temporal or eternal. However painful they may appear, troubles are a part of life in a world that was not designed for us initially, and it depends on how we handle them that determines whether we lose or retain glory that allows us to live free and happy lives. Humanity goes through troubles for one reason or another: as a repercussion for sins and to reveal God's mighty power (Hosea 4:4-9).

The Enemy of souls comes to steal and destroy us because he envies the fact that we have a great prospect of returning to glory. The undetected storms like the events of September 11 are examples of how Satan uses people and circumstances to launch a direct line of attack on humanity. In all the other cases, humanity has a part to play in our troubling circumstances as we wonder off in sin, flounder in ignorance and fail to go on the offense against the enemy. However, the underlying problem takes its root when we allow ourselves to become lured away subtly from paths of righteousness by the enemy. The only exception to that rule is when God wants to display His mighty power so that the enemy may know who reigns such was the case of Job.

God only allowed Satan to taunt Job because He wanted to prove to His defeated foe that humanity was, in fact, capable of remaining faithful to Him amid excruciating circumstances. Accusers of the truth are many because Satan uses tools like bigotry, racism, terrorism, backbiters, liars, hypocrites and barbarism in the hands of his agents to plague our minds. He is always active when God is at work within us and when we are rendering unto God our full benevolence. Agents of Satan are people who do not surrender their will to God; thus, they allow Satan to use them to carry out evil deeds against humanity and place fear in hearts. Knowing that his time is short, Satan wants to cut us off in unrighteousness before Christ finishes His intercessory work on our behalf. Satan has a personal vendetta with destiny to shake us down and sift us like wheat until we lose faith, hope and love. If not careful, we may become deceived because the great deceiver is at work in full force in our world today, dispatching agents who are willing to sacrifice their lives for his cause. People are eagerly sacrificing their lives, compromising their virtues and yielding their standards for some inexplicable trade-off. Nevertheless, God has put within us power to defy the enemy (Mark 16:17). In spite of the cause for troubles, we must be cognizant of who is our real enemy because Satan is the driving force behind all our problems.

It is *not* enough to know why troubles plague us but to understand how well we must manage them when they come, for they serve as part of the refining and purifying process through which our characters are perfected. All those who want temporal or a prospect of eternal glory must endure this process to win the victory. However, many of us miss out on the blessings that influence ultimate glory because we are too quick to run, hide, retaliate or reciprocate. How we handle our troubles determine whether or not we can overcome them. When we run, hide, retaliate or reciprocate, we cheat ourselves out of the purification process that brings healing; this can destroy our prospect of attaining ultimate glory. One of my favorite pastime quotes by Marcel Proust says, *"We are healed of a suffering only by experiencing it in full."* That approach suggests that we have to embrace the opportunity to face our troubles head-on. It simply implies that weak, passive and deceptive people have slim chances of being victorious. We can hope, but it is not enough to help us stand up against the wiles of the enemy, for Satan sends trouble to plague us to sift us like wheat so that he may confound and confuse us. However, God permits troubles to perfect our character because through the purification process we may learn patience, tolerance, faith and hope; these are traits conducive for glorious living.

For a long time, I cheated myself of the purification process brought about by unexpected trouble. There was one particular time in my life that I remember trying to evade the refining process. Obviously, I had habits: behaviors, personality traits and cultural barriers that God wanted me to break down before beginning His work in me. While I was still a very sheltered teenager, I experienced the loss of a dear uncle who was very close to me and still in the prime of his life.

Before I could manage that tragedy, I lost a cousin and then my dad. The losses of these three significant men in my life within a period of three years were unbearable! Nonetheless, I had the audacity to pretend I was cool, too cool to cry, so I thought that by not viewing their faces it would help. I wasn't about to show any vulnerability by mourning, so I played it—putting on a tough persona trying to manipulate my friends and family into thinking I wasn't weak. I managed to fool them successfully, pretending that I was doing okay. However, I couldn't fool myself for too long. It's always easy to deceive others but hard to feign self for any extended period.

My cousin's death had more of an impact on me than I realized. My initial reaction to it was denial, shock and then rebellion. Because of the unusual nature of his premature death, I shifted my pain towards family members, blaming some for his suicidal death. Later, I began having guilt feelings about my inability to prevent his death. Occasionally, I slipped in and out of questioning God and lost faith in Him briefly as I doubted His doings, but He obviously winked at me in the time of my ignorance.

After my dad died, all the unexpressed emotions from the past seemed to climax. Every time my emotions overwhelmed me, I would hide my heartache behind a smile or run and bury my sorrows in some activities, friends or family, but it didn't stop the hurt. I was hurting more badly than I wanted to admit. A family friend, an ex-mental health professional, tried to encourage me to cry, but I would not let up. Instead, I laughed for my peers. Early the morning after my dad's death, voices of sympathizers woke me up. As I tried to get to the bathroom, I ran into a crowd of people standing in the hallway. To work my way through the crowd, I had to shout, "excuse me, excuse me!" All eyes were on me at that time causing me some discomfort. A voice broke the cold silence as one lady asked, "How are you holding up?" I responded, "Well!" Then she exclaimed, "You are not holding up well at all. I can see that you were crying. Look how red and swollen your eye lids are." I was embarrassed but shocked because I didn't recall crying that night. I thought to myself, "I must have cried in my sleep." Denial got the better part of me, so to further cover up what I couldn't control I got a pair of sunshades.

Dad's death was a catharsis for my buried emotions. A few weeks after playing miss "tough" and "cool girl," my health started to suffer. After experiencing a series of intense headaches, my mom brought in our health and fitness director to check my blood pressure, which of course was normal. Yet, something abnormal was going on inside of me; something was causing discomfort. The painful headaches served as the beginning of my problems. For months thereafter, I constantly struggled with physical symptoms that one doctor diagnosed as acute laryngitis. However, other doctors ran several tests only to find that I was physically okay. After months of suffering, I knew that something was going on!

A few months after my dad's death, I visited my older sister in Canada attempting to get my life back together—to a state of normalcy. While there, I looked at the possibility of pursuing my higher education in Canada, but God had some work to do with me first. While I was there, I made some friends and got involved in all kinds of physical activities to keep my mind at ease. The grandmother of one of my closest friends, Antoinette, got very sick. For some time, there was no diagnosis about the cause of her sickness; but one day, I accompanied her to the hospital and became very suspicious about the nature of her grandmother's sickness. After watching my father losing his two-year fight to cancer, I became an expert on the symptoms of this deadly disease. However, I did not want to disturb Antoinette by sharing my suspicions with her because she had bright hopes. The next time we visited, her grandmother shared with us the diagnosis; I was right on target! Hearing the diagnosis produced an uncontrollable emotional reaction that led me to abandon Antoinette. I could not be there for her when she needed me the most. I was too vulnerable from the hurts of my own troubled past to strengthen her, so I left the room to find a nice little quiet place where I could vent my emotions. It wasn't long before my friend's grandmother lost her battle to cancer. I knew Antoinette was hurting badly, yet I felt helpless because there was not much I could do in my current vulnerable state.

One day, another friend told me about a grief recovery seminar that was going on, and I took Antoinette to help her find the resolve she needed, never thinking that I needed such therapy—No, I'm too cool! What transpired at that seminar that day changed my life forever; for the better. To begin the session, the psychologist introduced himself and gave a personal testimony and then encouraged everyone to do likewise but not until after he mentioned acceptance as the first stage of grief recovery. He encouraged everyone to share a personal experience. The first person's experience struck a nerve inside me. I could relate to her painful experience and identify with her hurt, but I was still a bit ignorant about why I was there, for my friend and *not* me.

Before long, I began experiencing a lump-like symptom inside my back. By the time the second person began talking, I felt like the lump was growing. It grew bigger and bigger until it felt like it was gradually working its way up my back until it lodged itself inside my throat. For a minute, I thought I was dying. Once there, the lump like symptom kept pressing me until I felt like it was about to explode. It took me a while before I heard anything that anyone was saying because I was so preoccupied with that terrible feeling. Somehow, a lady began talking, and it was just as if she had raised her voice so loud that I could not overlook what she was saying. I could identify with her painful experience, and my tears began to overwhelm me as I tried to choke them back, but this time I could not stop the flow of tears down my face. The psychologist got used to handing out a tissue to each person that was sobbing; when he came up to me, he handed me the entire box of tissues. I tried to stop my tears, but they were uncontrollable. All the calmness I felt when I walked into that room disappeared. I couldn't escape the emotions that overwhelmed me because I was too embarrassed to call any unnecessary attention to myself as tears kept gushing out. I wanted to scream loudly to relieve the trapped feeling I had inside, but pride interfered.

From that point on, it was difficult for me to hear what anyone else was sharing. I wanted to talk but feared losing total control of my emotions. By the time the session was over, I felt more relieved. Before I left, I hugged all those who shared their stories. When I left the room that day, I felt as if the weight of the world had fallen off my shoulders. All those prior problems I experienced before seemed to have disappeared permanently. My tears, the very tears I tried so hard to hide, became an outlet—cleansing away the choked up pain that came with the unexpected turmoil. These personal losses all within one year had profound lasting negative effects on my physiological and psychological well being for years. I took on a negative outlook, which I later realized affected my relationship with others, leading me to withdraw from my friends and family members who were closest to me. Although I withdrew because I was afraid of losing those I love, breaking down the bonds of closeness didn't bring me any closure to the pain stemming from the deaths of my Uncle, Cousin and Dad.

What I discovered that day was that regardless of how long we go through difficulties, we will never begin to heal until we take a proactive step to accept our troubles, handling them gracefully without self-deception or maliciously hurting others. Our degree of healing is dependent on whether we are optimistic or not. How we deal with our troubles can dictate how quickly we are healed and restored back to normalcy. In a famous quote Aristotle said, *"Suffering becomes beautiful when anyone bears calamities with cheerfulness, not through insensibility but through greatness of mind."* Our character is perfected when we go through the storms and pain of trouble or become kindled by the flames of God's fire. As normally happens, when humans become complacent, we harden our hearts to God and others, stray from paths of righteousness or become offended when we are corrected. Sometimes it takes a bitter blow—a rude awakening from God to wake us up and get us out of our comfort zone, but such an awakening can have positive results. It can serve to correct, direct, inspect, perfect and protect us. At times when our batteries die out, God has to light a fire to recharge us. Other times God sees us trying to please Him, and He wants to inspect us—test us to see what's deep within us. He knows, but He wants to show us whether we are the sincere Christians we profess. He wants to know how much of the anointed oil we have absorbed. Thus, he places us in a situation like a woman placed under the heat of hair drier. She wants to have her hair relaxed with the right oil, which requires that her head have enough heat for the oil to be saturated. The heat God places us in is an opportunity for the Spirit to saturate our being.

God wants to perfect our characters, for He sees that living in this environment of sin has caused us to take on personalities, attitudes and characters that would deny us temporal and eternal glory. These heated opportunities help us understand that the things we love and hold dear to our hearts were just given to us for a little while and now we can allow His beauty to be seen in us. God wants us to understand that the real glory lies ahead, and we should not get too caught up in moments of instant gratification or the cares of this world. There are, however, times when God wants to correct us when He see us straying from His precepts, not taking seriously our moral obligations to Him, others and ourselves (taking care of our bodies—His living temple). He loves us and wants us to change our lives around after we have gone astray, so He can bring back our glory.

Personally, I received many benefits from dealing with my painful past. If God didn't allow me to go through these circumstances and I did not position myself to receive His chastisement, my character wouldn't have been refined. Those very painful experiences helped me to see myself as God sees me, wretched and undone, and that positioned me to grow and develop into the wonderful person that I am becoming. Only after putting away deception, retaliation and pride did I gradually begin to heal. I now know that God is not lurking around waiting to see what I have done wrong so that He can punish. That harsh image I had of God earlier in my life as my trials soared disappeared as I drew closer to Him. The more obstacles I overcame, the more positive I became. Dealing with troubles in an honest and open way helped me become more optimistic, appreciate those around me more and hold those closest to me with high regards.

Today, I live a freer and happier life as I remind myself not to mask or manipulate, which are both deceptive behaviors, to gain the favor of others or influence them. My troubles made me more sympathetic to the needs of others and compassionate to those that go through something. Now I know what trouble means and have a greater appreciation for the needs of others. These days, I am better prepared to deal with the realities of life and more spiritually awakened. I now see my troubles as an opportunity for

God to perfect my character and allow him to begin the transformation process that will enable me to see His true purpose and plan for glorious living. Despite what others may say or how we feel, I find that the longer we stay in an environment of sin, the more sin becomes prominent in our lives and that is what people will see instead of the beauty of God's glory that should shine forth from within. It is God's will that we are willful about reaching for greater glory at all costs.

Troubles affect us most profusely when we are resistant to change and when we condone behaviors that has no significant bearing in the presence of God's glory. By holding on to things, habits, attitudes and behaviors that draw us away from godliness and righteousness, regardless how innocent or insignificant they may seem, puts us out of focus (reach) and out of alignment to receive greater glory. People get caught up in wrong deeds because they haven't found themselves; thus, they feel discomfort and unease that draws them into actions that causes grief, heartache and pain. Those who do not position themselves for God's glory get caught off guard when unforeseen storms and pain come. This throws them into disparagement and robs them of their temporal glory. A life is in turmoil when it is in the wrong position, and the only way to get back in focus is to reach for greater glory. Reaching positions us for God to see something good within us that will move Him to act in our favor and put us within glorious realms. All those who position themselves for greater glory develop a faith that will not shrink when it is pressed by many foes, allowing them to bounce back into a rightful spirit quickly after unexpected storms and pain are experienced. Thus, they can enjoy the rewards of living gloriously.

Chapter 5

THE COST OF EXECUTING OUR FREE WILL

The right to execute our free will is inherently ours, but it doesn't come without a cost: giving up self-gratification and instant gratification. Neither is the right to execute our free will without its reward—glory, both temporal and eternal. A glorious outcome is one of balance we experience when we align or position ourselves with the Creator, His creation, others and ourselves. The desired outcome of glory is a life filled with peace, joy, hope and harmony. This outcome does not come without a cost.

Adam and Eve were the first two human beings who got to execute their free wills; unfortunately, they chose to disobey God despite being made perfect beings. As a result, they lost their glory, and humanity has had to pay the price for their sin. On the other hand, Job—a man that was born in sin and shaped in iniquity, stood his ground in opposition to fulfilling his own selfish ambition. Job could have chosen to never love again after his beloved wife told him to curse God and die, as well as his friends turning their backs against him. Instead of going his own way as a fallen and defeated man to die in his sin, he chose to execute his free will. By following after righteousness and reaching for greater glory, God rewarded him justly by bringing back his temporal glory. Job, in addition, received double fold of all that he had lost for his troubles.

The choices we make every day determine the price we must pay as well as the reward we receive. When we choose to identify with God, we make good choices, which lead to works of righteousness; these are works that have the best spiritual, mental, and physical interest of others in mind (Isaiah 58). These actions bring intrinsic rewards of making one fully human and vitally alive. As stated by Isaiah the prophet, *"And the work of righteousness shall be peace; and the effect of righteousness quietness and assurance forever"* (Isaiah 32:17). However, we automatically choose to identify with the forces of evil when we make decisions that are self-serving, following the way of Lucifer, now called Satan (Isaiah 14:4-15). Although Adam and Eve chose that path, we can choose to execute our free wills like Job and change our course in life. Unless we turn away from evil, the experience of glory: joy, peace, hope and harmony—oneness with the Creator—are impossible. As noted in *The Original African Heritage Bible* in a footnote regarding Isaiah 32:17:

> *...This proverb expresses that righteousness is the main element of peace. Therefore, it is in vain for men to think peace can be achieved if there is no effort to change their evil ways. It is vain to constantly preach peace without any righteous works to manifest it. Something must be done continuously by those who*

> *profess to desire peace. Their righteous*
> *works will be the determining factor if their*
> *desire for peace is sincere (Winston, John*
> *C. 1036)*[1]

The advantage of executing our free will indicates that we can design our own course of actions, alter our fate or design our prospect of glory. Believe it or not, we are all spiritual beings. That means that we are all contenders in the great controversy, the battle against good and evil; the side we choose will dictate our fate. Those who choose to do works of righteousness will reap blessings and rewards, but those who choose to walk in self-glory and unrighteousness will pay the ultimate devastating price and reap negative consequences. Any one who wants to stay impartial may be in for a rude awakening because there is no middle ground. Satan will not fail to attempt to influence each one of us, especially those who profess God, to deny our Creator. He wants us to view God's commandments as bogus, harsh and arbitrary. What we must be cognizant of is that a moment of sinful pleasure is not worth a lifetime of doom. We cannot experience God's glory in our lives if we don't execute our free will in a way that is spiritually right.

Anytime we allow Satan to intervene, God cannot come to our rescue uninvited; we have to reach for greater glory. That means reaching is a crucial step. In His love, God must allow us to execute our free will to choose between what is wrong and right even though He knows that the path we have decided may lead to total destruction. He does all that is possible, short of making our decision, to prevent destruction of various forms. If a form of destruction occurs while still living, we have to find our way back into His good graces, surrendering our will to Him by unconditionally inviting Him back into our hearts to heal and restore.

Through the ages, God always had moral heroes, and He still has them now. Joseph, Elijah and Daniel are perfect examples of heroes from the past who were not ashamed to acknowledge themselves as His peculiar people. In our modern day, God still has heroes; strong men and women, boys and girls and even children in our generation who are willing to stand up for what is right regardless of popular opinion or what seems enticing. The choices we make prepare us for the battles we face. By putting things in perspective early in our lives we brace ourselves internally so that we do not betray God. Refusing the sinful pleasure and allurements of the world, we may have to endure afflictions because Satan knows our weaknesses and will press hard upon them, but we must rest assured that God will work things out for our good like He did for those in times past.

By choosing to respond negatively or insensitively to others regardless of who they are or what they have done, we reap negative consequences. When decisions are made that run contrary to divine principles, we will eventually reap shame, guilt, and pain; these adverse consequences are what God wants to deliver us from and to save us unto a life of rightness with Him and those around us. Too often, when we make poor decisions and make it a habit, we lose sight of the source of such a habit. Some of us perform acts that lead to pain; such acts turn into bad habits, and those habits become our lifestyle. To reverse the lifestyle requires four things: face the problem, trace the problem, embrace the problem, and erase the problem. David sinned miserably, but with a contrite heart his attitude was corrected. First, he faced the problem by acknowledging his transgression that his actions were a deliberate and premeditated willful violation of a divine norm. Secondly, he traced the problem back to sin, recognizing that because of his actions he missed the mark and deviated from God's precepts. Thirdly, he embraced the problem, accepting that it was a result of his own iniquity—his crookedness and perverse behavior. Finally, he erased the problem by confessing his fault of deceptiveness in his attempt to cover up and evade his evil act. David was able to place himself in a position for divine forgiveness allowing the Spirit of Holiness to cleanse his inner being.

Reversing of lifestyle is no easy or immediate process, but it is possible and necessary in order to position oneself to begin receiving the glory, which was lost as a result of sin. Initially, glory was lost in the garden for humanity as a whole. Then, more temporal glory was lost by conditioning as a child to fit into an imperfect environment that was created by flawed human beings: parental, biologically or psychologically authorities. Like David, we must learn how to get to the source of that which causes us to lose our glory then execute our free will to manage it by ultimately erasing it, so it no longer has a negative impact that robs us of peace and harmony with the Creator. The whole concept of the Hebrew sanctuary ritual is putting negative things back on the original source (Lev.16: 5-10, 14-22—particularly from the *Clear Word Bible*). God can bring back His glory if we turn away from evil, *"for the Lord knoweth the way of the righteous; but the way of the ungodly shall perish"* (Psalm 1:6 NEB). We have to remember that *"Where sin increased, grace increased all the more, so that, just as sin reigned in death, so also grace might reign through righteousness to bring eternal life through Jesus Christ our Lord"* (Romans 5:20, 21 NIV).

God has given us a special privilege—the freedom to choose whether to continue living in evil or righteousness (right living with Him and fellow human beings), so we can't ultimately blame anyone for our consequences. As a child, a local singer sang a song that said, *"the evil that men do live after them."* If that holds true, then we should do good today to avoid unnecessary hurt and shame in the future. If we must suffer, it should be for good and not evil because the sufferings we endure for good will not go unrewarded. Whether we make right or wrong choices is dependent on our relationship with God or his foe, Satan. We must be cognizant that Satan is the driving force behind all bad actions, and he will hold true to his purpose of reaping havoc on our souls if we don't reconcile to God before it is too late. This havoc robs us of our glory that is available even right now.

When we are at our lowest, it seems that we tend to draw closer to God. Tragedies place us in a position to call on God. Orison Swett Marden, American author and founder of *Success Magazine* said, *"Obstacles are like wild animals. They are cowards, but they will bluff you if they can. If they see you are afraid of them... they are liable to spring upon you; but... if you look them squarely in they eye, they will slink out of sight."* We can run but can't hide from the realities of troubles. It is more worthwhile to face them head-on until we conquer them.

Troubles force us to turn to God in prayer for strength, which enable us to weather the storms and manage the pain. Unforeseen disasters serve as a spiritual wake up call for those who choose not to see happenings from a spiritual perspective. Many of us would continue to sleep walk with our eyes wide open had it not been for wake up calls. While tragedies remind us of our vulnerabilities, it causes us to feel a great need for a Savior. The dilemma is whether we will choose to yield to God or continue to take matters in our own hands. God permits bad things to happen for our greater good; He does not desire that we experience the full brunt of evil. Unfortunately, when we experience tragedies, we act without thinking; we jump to conclusions about the tragedies rather than to step back and look back again to see what is not obvious to the casual observer.

Aristotle once said that, *"an unexamined life is not a life worth living."* So it is in our spiritual lives or any other aspect of our existence. We must choose to examine our plight to better manage it to see how it can be used for a better purpose. As complacent people, oftentimes, it takes a bitter blow to wake us up, but the blow can produce positive results. It can correct, direct, perfect, protect us. Like gold, we must be tried in the fire to get rid of any dross and other impurities. Fire is not comfortable but well needed. Once we have been tried, the value of our experience is likened to a priceless jewel or a sincere friend who is precious and rare. We will experience storms, but it is our choice how we handle those storms.

We cannot allow others to dictate how we execute our free will, for it is a precious gift from God that only we must give account for. What we must do is stand up for what is right and let others know what we stand for and what we don't stand for even though it is not popular. Mary H. Waldrip said it best, *"It's important that people should know what you stand for. It's equally important that they know what you won't stand for."* When we stand for what is right, we take courage and become strong to win the victory over evil and temptation, with the love of Christ constraining us. By electing to obey God and choosing our companions with care, He in turn redefines our relationships—bringing good people into our lives to bless us. This not only empowers us but also enables us to fulfill our earthly destiny and gives us a foretaste of the joys of God's divine glory.

Although sometimes we go against spiritual laws that bring negative consequences, God in His grace and mercy can save us from those natural consequences. Sometimes it takes His performing a miracle. This is not to say that He goes against the spiritual or even natural laws; rather He introduces a new law, which transcends what He previously established, and He performs the impossible. Even when our holy and just God allows us to pay the consequences, He already has a plan in place to reconcile us back to Himself after we go astray. However, it requires that we choose to *"seek good and not evil"* so that we may live (Amos 5:14 RSV). God can still restore us if we ask His forgiveness, confess our faults to one another, confess our sins to Him, and repent from our evil ways. What God wants is to turn His people into a saving relationship with Him. He wants us to learn from the past, to deal with the past, to face the past, to embrace the past and then to erase the past. He does not desire that we live in the past no matter how bad or how good it may have been. Confession helps us to deal with the past and to move beyond it.

Imagine the courage it took for tennis star, Monica Seles to face her fears after a deranged fan stabbed her in 1993; wounds barely missed her spinal cords! No doubt she was haunted by the memories of this incident for a longtime. While in the hospital, she couldn't stop asking, "what if he comes back?" Imagine her horrors after a judge released her assailant on a two years' probation. She was so harassed by those gruesome images that left an impression on her mind. Only by executing her free will wisely, by making a true confession to a psychologist about her fears and pain, could Monica win the victory; with the support and encouragement of her friends and family, she could move on. Thus, she learned from the past, to deal with the past, to face the past, to embrace the past and then to erase the painful memory of the past. True confessions free us from the pain that weighs down on our souls by releasing us of the burdens of past painful experiences. When we look back on the situation, we can feel at ease; as we look back, we can learn from the past to rise above it.

Monica had a bad past, but even a good past can prevent us from moving forward into the God's glory. When a casual reader looks at Isaiah 43:18-19, he might think that Israel had a bad past going on: "Forget the former things; do not dwell on the past. See I am doing a new thing! Now it springs up; do you not perceive it? I am making a way in the desert and streams in the wasteland" (New International Version). However, when these two verses are placed in context, the reader realizes that Israel had a good past. Israel was created by God—good; Israel was redeemed by God—good; Israel was named by God—good; God brought them through the waters— good; God brought them through the fire—good; God gave them land—good; God gathered their children from the Diaspora—good; God secures them—good (Isaiah 43:1-17). Yet, the LORD of Creation tells Israel to forget it all. Whether our past is bad or good, if we do not move beyond it to the greater glory ahead, we will become entangled in old victories when new victories are needed. God expects loyalty of everyone that He has created; it is a loyalty to live life fully and gloriously. He will give us the power according to our needs to walk upright. However, in our own strength we can do nothing but in God's might, for he is strong enough to enable us to choose to overcome evil.

The LORD does not want us dangling in the past, good or bad, for it destroys our present prospects and darkens our future glory. God wants us to see that He has so much more to reveal to us each day, so many more miracles to perform for us, so many more blessings to shower down on us. He wants us to be aware that when it comes to what He can do, "we ain't seen nothin' yet." *But as it is written, Eye hath not seen, nor ear heard, neither have entered into the heart of man, the things which God hath prepared for them that love Him"* (1 Corinthians 2:9). It is an exercise of our will to love God and follow after His righteousness and receive Him that we are saved from those natural consequences to reap those rewards.

In the parable of the seed, Christ makes reference to two categories of people that received the word in stony places and became unfruitful. The first is about those who are not rooted in God that become offended when tribulation or persecution comes because of not being grounded in the word. A second group of people are those that receive or hear the word but allow the cares of this world and the deceitfulness of riches to choke out the word (Matthew 13:21,22). The group that really mattered to Him included those who received the word on good ground—hearing the word, understood it and brought forth fruit (vs. 23). Those who seek out a church or friendships for comfort, size, compromising message or values, to gain social status or approval are among the group that Christ referred to as seeds that fell on stony ground because they experience things which choke out the word of God. They are neither convicted nor bring forth fruit. Neutrality is halting between two opinions; by choosing to stay neutral we automatically reject God's word. John tells us in his book of Revelation that in the final analysis, God will spew out of His mouth neutrals—people that can't make up their mind about who they want to serve or which side they are on (3:16).

It doesn't matter what transpired in the past or what lies ahead, the choice is ours to live faithfully by spiritual standards or to become swayed by material gain and popular opinion. We must remember that the things we love and hold dear to our hearts may come between God and us. They come easily, but just as easily as they come they can also quickly be taken from us for they are not ours, in the end. God only lets us use them to brighten our way, and sometimes He has to remind us of that fact. If we choose to live faithfully, we will be brave, kind, strong and true. Thus, it doesn't matter what lies ahead; we can face it head on with confidence knowing that God will keep us in perfect peace if our minds are stayed upon Him (Isaiah 26:3). God holds our future in the palm of His hand, and He won't fail us when bad times come along bringing hurt and pain.

We have to realize that without God we can do nothing, and by choosing to commit ourselves to do only what He expects of us every moment of every day is to return to our glory. When we yield our lives to God completely, He can begin the refining process in our lives to mold us and make us after His will. To retain our glory, we need the Prince of Peace to guide our free wills. When Christ comes into our hearts, we will be at ease because He bids our fears and doubts away. The peace we need comes from oneness with God and is available if we can pray:

> Prince of peace, control my will,
> Bid the struggling heart be still;
> Bid the fears and doubting cease,
> Hush my spirit into peace.
>
> Thou hast bought me with thy blood,
> Opened wide the gate to God;
> Peace, I ask, but peace must be,
> Lord, in being one with Thee.
>
> May Thy will, not mine, be done,
> May Thy will and mine be one;
> Chase the doubtings from my heart,
> Now Thy perfect peace impart.[2]

Even though our Prince of Peace can not control our will, we can choose which side we are on in the spiritual warfare and stand ready for action because choosing to fight on the offensive doesn't mean that we are not going to become drawn into a conflict. Whether we profess to be soldiers in God's army or not, we all have to fight on one side or the other, so we need to stand ready for action. If we don't choose which side we are on, it will be automatically determined for us. Just like how President George W. Bush declared as he prepared to launch the war against terrorism, "you are either with us or against us" so God sees us. There is no middle ground in this spiritual warfare. We have to stand for what is right and do what is right or risk falling for anything. All of us have to make clear distinctions which side we are on and stand ready for action as we raise our standards because if we are not standing on guard, in watchfulness, we may be taken off guard and forced to defend ourselves in enemy territory.

There is a war between good and evil; God is the driving force behind all good actions and delights in right doings; on the other hand, Satan is the originator of evil and every wrong act, regardless of how innocent it appears, is orchestrated by the same spirit that caused him to rebel and be cast out of the glorious presence of the Creator. It doesn't matter who's committing evil, what side one takes dictates which side that individual is fighting on. Not declaring to be a soldier of God, we automatically choose to side with evil. If we choose God's side then we choose to do that which is good and follow after works of righteousness, those things that are characteristically synonymous to the fruits of the spirit: love, joy, peace, longsuffering, gentleness, goodness, faith, meekness and temperance (Galatians 5:22,23). By siding, embracing and supporting evildoers, we choose to fight on the enemy's side. Just like there are distinct boundaries in the physical warfare, so there are distinct differences in the choices we make.

Good intentions never gain us any favor in the fight against good and evil, instead it shrinks our reach of glory. If we sow works of righteousness, we will reap rewards; if we sow iniquity, we shall reap negative consequences. No matter how special we think we are, God's Word applies to each of us equally. If we are not prepared for warfare physically, spiritually, mentally and emotionally our good intentions will not suffice. It can cause us to lose our glory.

Christ points us to the glory we need to help us execute our free will in ways that bring rewards. He died to give us the power to rise above our frailties, so we can make wiser decisions. Even if it is not popular, we have to stand our ground knowing that one person empowered by Christ can defy an evil army. This may not sound realistic but look at the heroes in the Bible, in particular Elijah. In his own strength, he could not escape the wrath of Jezebel coupled with the 450 priests of Baal, but he kept on standing up for what was right and God delivered him. When we open up our heart to the Savior, He will come in and transform our lives. All of us, like sheep have gone astray far from the glory of God's presence, but we can make ourselves accessible again to become fashioned after His divine will. Inside of us there is a sweet Holy Spirit that is telling us which way to go. When we tap into the Spirit, the prophet Isaiah says that our ears will hear a word behind us saying, *"This is the way, walk in it"* (Isaiah 30:21). Trying to execute our free will on our own leads to utter failure, but God's Spirit will always direct us to take the right path.

The battle between good and evil, the great controversy, is partly fought between human agencies—those that seek to do good and those who choose to do evil. The question is, "who will we serve?" How we answer this question will determine whether we lose or win. None of us can win if we focus on ourselves. The only way to win is by focusing on Christ's righteousness and His saving grace. We must follow Christ for He says, *"I am the way, the truth, and the life: no man cometh unto the Father but by me"* (John 14:6). Without Christ leading our lives, we are like a ship without a sail, drifting and tossing on troubled waters. Only Christ can free us from the bondage of sin so that we can live hopeful, joyful, peaceful and harmonious lives. Thus, the value of executing a spirit-led free will is like a priceless treasure or a friendship that is precious but rare as is God's divine glory that we all need to seek and find.

To execute one's free will in a way that pleases God is to position oneself to reach and receive greater glory. One who is wise will position oneself for that glory because the rewards far outweigh the short-lived feelings of self-gratification or instant gratification.

Chapter 6

ARMED TO RECEIVE GREATER GLORY

When one chooses to receive the temporal glory that will lead to eternal glory, he or she must be prepared for battle because there's a war going on in this earth. Though Christ has already won the ultimate battle at the cross, the war continues to rage for other contenders, the righteous and all their adversaries will carry on until He returns to bring back the ultimate glory by bringing an end to all enmity. Preparation for claiming or attaining the victory requires a willful act; ironically, the willful act requires submission to a greater WILL who has both our best interest at heart and the best interest of the rest of humanity. Victory cannot convene without a physical and spiritual battle—a war!

Any casual observer will recognize that humanity at both the collective and individual levels gets mixed up in battles—war against ours mind, against others and against spiritual beings. While some battles can be expected, others flare up unexpectedly; these take us off guard. When we begin to exercise our free wills, we will realize that many battles can be anticipated, managed, and minimized. However, exercising our free will requires trust to yield our will to someone far greater who can oversee the larger war picture—the entire battlefield. This person is someone who not only has a wider view of the battle but also has a greater experience in fighting and winning the battle. Before going into the need of submitting our will to a greater WILL, it is important to understand what a war involves.

A war is any type of confrontation that seeks to violate a person and keep him from receiving the opportunity to become fully human and vitally alive. War constitutes an external (physical) or internal (mental/spiritual) confrontation where one party does not care to recognize what's in the best interest of another person. A war is a confrontation that ignores the sacredness of life for individuals or a group of individuals. There are those who claim that some wars must be fought; thus, they're justified. However, there are those who oppose wars. Archbishop Desmond Tutu, 1984 Nobel Peace Prize recipient, posed several questions regarding war in an interview with Anne M. Simpkinson:

> *"Is there such a thing as a just war? The just war theory was a recognition that we live in a less-than-perfect world. In an ideal world, there ought to be no war, for war is evil—but it might be the lesser of two evils. It might be better to go to war against Hitler than to allow him to throw babies into gas ovens. There were criteria to be satisfied before the serious and ugly business is undertaken: Have you exhausted all possible peaceful alternatives? Will you,*

if war is declared, abide by the conventions governing conflict; namely, that you target only the military?

I agree that most wars can be avoided and the number of casualties can be minimized. This concept of war is applicable to the physical realm of existence as well as the mental and spiritual realms. The real war is not between people but between spiritual beings; people are spiritual beings because we have a spiritual force that dwells within our hearts. We do not fight against flesh and blood although many of the wars manifest themselves through physical channels. Contrary to what many think, when we fight wars, there is a driving force behind all our motives that determines whether we seek good or evil.

The September 11, 2001 atrocity was a physical act of war, but it was merely the manifestation of something much deeper. Thus, physical retaliation is insufficient to combat the war on terrorism. Terrorism, like any other form of war, is tangible evidence of people experiencing inner struggles; hurt people! Unspiritual people do unspiritual things. Undisciplined people reap the consequences of a haphazard and dangerous life. Unless we become soldiers in the battle for the spiritual wellbeing of those around us and ourselves, we'll continue to become victims of warfare—terror-fare! It wasn't shocking to realize that the American government understood the concept of behaving in a way that was honorable when they provided a humanitarian effort to help hurting people before they initially declared and pursued war on terrorism in Afghanistan. While at both the individual and collective levels, we must anticipate and experience war in both the physical and spiritual realms. "Although there is a difference between physical warfare and spiritual warfare, there is still a close relationship. In fact, all physical warfare is part of the spiritual war" (Read James 4 and 2 Peter 2:11). The question here is not whether or not we are going to war but how are we going to prepare to fight our spiritual and physical warfare?

Both spiritual and physical warfare must be fought offensively and defensively (II Corinthians10:5). IN WARFARE, the offensive is the means by which one takes the objective. It is an aggressive advance against an enemy to wrestle the objective from his possession (e.g. USA against Iraq for Kuwait). An army on the offensive has a moral and physical advantage over the enemy at the point of contact. The offensive is both an attitude as well as direction. In attitude, it is bold; in direction it is a forward advance towards the enemy at the objective; as its means it uses effective weapons. However, the defensive is the means by which one reacts to a previous attack that was launched against him. A good example of such is the war against terrorism where America and its allies are fighting back by raging war on Osama Bin Laden and those they believe are responsible or supportive of the attacks on the financial and military headquarters. Effective fighting requires the ability to be on the defense and on the offense.

In the spiritual war, a defensive is conducted in response to an attacking subject and directed against the enemy, not against the objective. Satan is the enemy. He has tried several times to defeat God and is constantly warring against humanity to try and undermine God's authority. We fight in order to wrest from his possession those who through fear of death are subject to his bondage. According to Hebrews 2:15, most of this spiritual war is already history. Jesus Christ delivered the decisive blow at the absolute point at the definitive time. The blow was His death for sin to redeem sinners; the point was a cross outside the city of Jerusalem, and the time was the feast of the Passover about A.D. 30. The Bible reveals that the blow destroyed the enemy and set prisoners free. What remains as the decisive blow has been struck! We must proclaim the emancipation to Satan's captives. We must declare the means of freedom, the gospel, the defeat of Satan, and the victory of Christ through His death and resurrection. We must participate in that ancient victory, for its proclamation is still unfinished. It is still news, which many captives have not heard.

In the spiritual war the offensive is carried out by two very basic means: *preaching* and *prayer.* Preaching, when done in the power of the Holy Spirit is an engagement on a spiritual plane. Other powers are in conflict beside the speaker and the listeners. In 2 Timothy chapter 2, we can see four participants in the conflict: the LORD 's servant, the opponent, God and the Devil. We take the offensive under orders, praying and preaching in the Holy Spirit (Acts 5: 20; 1Timothy 2:1-6; Ephesians 6: 18-20; Matthew 9: 37,38). Our objective is encouraging and supporting people. The enemy holds them captive at his own will. Then let us move out; let us advance toward the objective, praying and preaching." Some special tools are needed to endure the spiritual warfare (A. Othniel).

To fight defensively or offensively in the spiritual warfare and win, we have to reach for greater glory;

which calls for putting on the whole armor of God. Special weaponry is needed: essential tools that are necessary to fight and win in our spiritual warfare against Satan and his agents. Confidence is good, but every good soldier knows that being overly confident in one's individual ability can lead to neglect or lack of preparedness. When fighting in the defensive or offensive warfare, one has to wear gear every day or risk being taken off guard. Like so many have done before, a true Soldier must not make the mistake of relying on his own strength or skillfulness to get through the storms and pain in life. Comparing the parts of the authentic Roman soldier's armor with the spiritual armor of God may bring some awareness of the things we need to become successful in the spiritual war that is raging in and around our lives.

THE WHOLE ARMOR OF GOD			
PARTS OF THE ARMOR	**THE IMPORTANCE OF THE PART**	**WHAT THOSE PARTS REPRESENT**	**SUPPORTING SCRIPTURE**
BELT	Keep body armor in place	*TRUTH AND HONESTY*	Romans 4:15,25
BREASTPLATE	Sleeveless body armor: leader jacket, with metal strips sewn in	*RIGHTEOUSNESS:* Purity	Romans 5:3
SANDALS	Are worn on the feet. They are made of leather sole, tied by leather thongs up to the knee.	*GOSPEL OF PEACE:* Bringing unity among each other.	Romans 4:3
SHEILD	Rectangular in shape, thin layer of wood glued together, with bronze or iron edges	*FAITH:* Relying on God for strength	Romans 3:20 Psalm 3:3
HELMET	Bronze, with an inner Plate of iron, with protective extension for the back of the neck.	*SALVATION:* Being a part of Christ body keeps us safe since Christ is our Savior.	Eph. 6:17 Ps. 62:2,6
SWORD	Two-edged, 2 feet long, carried in a sheath	*THE SPIRIT:* The Word of God (Bible) is our weapon of attack.	Ephesians 6:17
WATCH-FULNESS	Perseverance and Supplication	*PRAYERFULLNESS:* Praying in the Spirit for all saints.	Ephesians 6:18

Some of the battles we engage in physically or spiritually are not the war of individual citizens. National and International wars are fought between entities which enlist individuals by any means necessary. The spiritual warfare is not ours to fight as human beings; it is the Lord's, and we are in this together because the stakes are high! (II Chronicle 20:15)

The Outcome of Internal/Spiritual War

There is a subtle internal spiritual war going on in this earth which began in heaven and has already been won at the cross. This is manifested basically as a war for human hearts and minds. Since the fall of man when the war came to earth, Satan has been fighting to control people's hearts and minds. Unlike the physical battle, which is fought with visible weaponry (bombs, bullets, chemicals guns, jets, tanks and technology) this battle is primarily fought out in silence—in the quiet recesses of our hearts and minds—the seat of human conscience. We cannot sit back in laxity fully dependent on Christ to fight all our battles; we have to reach out to Him to receive greater glory. However, we need weapons that will enable us to fight offensively and defensively against this most subtle of foes in this battle. To eliminate the potential of being eliminated when sin, death and Satan consume us, we must understand the nature of this conflict and the part we play in it to take advantage of the victory won for us by Christ on the cross. Our role is presently in I Peter 2: 9-12:

- **Aliens and strangers** (v.11): Since we are a holy nation, our citizenship is not of this world—we are aliens and strangers. It's not talking about location but our sinful lifestyle warring against the LORD. We speak a different language—the words of God. We eat different food—the milk of God's Word. We wear different clothes—the blood of the Lamb. We live differently—we don't retaliate, judge, give up, or mistreat others

- **Sinful desires** (v.11): We are addicts to sin. This means that we are to have a holy frustration. Frustration is the sign of a fighting soldier. If you are apathetic, it shows that you are not a soldier; you are a civilian.

- **Wage war** (v.11): Literally, "serve as a soldier." We are to fight. What is at stake? **Souls.** Not inconsequential things like that on the evening news but that which is important—souls. This is why we want the score to be 100-0 although 100-98 might be a good basketball score. Souls are precious, and these are what are at stake in this war. What is the *length* of the war? *All our lives.* What is our *weapon*? Good deeds.

- **Right heart.** Christianity is not only about *behavior modification* but *inner transformation.* A better question than *what is our weapon* is *who is God's weapon*? Men and women of God whose hearts are purified by the war of the soul.

- **War, accuse (v. 11, 12):** There are two kinds of battles: **Internal** or **sinful desires**. **External** or **people's accusations**.

- **<u>Glorify God</u> (v. 12):** The measure of victory is the glory of God. How can we measure our victory? How much was God glorified? How valuable is my life? How much do I glorify God?

This war between evil and good is addressed in not only the Christian faith but also all other faiths. Having a faith is to have some means of dealing with the spiritual war, which often manifests itself in the physical realm of our existence. Terrorism versus the United States of America best reveals the nature of the war at the physical level, which best exemplifies the war at the spiritual level. Terrorists seek their own good in the name of religion at the expense of anyone and everyone. They do not consider the people who may have little or no means to negotiate to avoid a conflict. It must be said that most wars of the world are terroristic to some extent. To distinguish between wars and terrorist acts, the former is a declared frontal attack whereas the latter is likened to unannounced guerilla warfare. Guerilla warfare thrives on deception, booby traps and vigilantism.

Other than the above distinction, both types of conflict are full of fatalism and leaves wounded soldiers who believe in the cause. Nevertheless, these conflicts have a way of taking our glory when we are not alert. Thus, it is unwise to take our enemy lightly as may have happened when people produced humorous animations and columns about Osama Bin Laden. They may make us laugh, but confrontation with such a personality can leave one quite devastated. Much like what happens when we take Satan lightly. Many have become casualties of the spiritual warfare because of either not taking him too seriously or not acknowledging him at all. Satan wants this of people, as does any enemy, because it allows him to take advantage of his prey when they are most vulnerable. Thus, the question is how does one avoid being taken advantage of in a guerilla warfare that one cannot tangibly see?

When we view life as a war, we will begin to live life differently; we will be more alert to stay on guard to protect what is vital to our existence and to ward off would be predators. Satan is the great predator, seeking to and fro, for whom he can devour. Like Olympic athletes, Christians are engaged in a war that requires rigorous preparation consisting of grueling tests in order to obtain the ultimate gold of glory. To obtain this gold requires a real recognition that our existence is one of wartime. With this in mind, we will understand the necessity of prayer as a major defensive and offensive weapon.

The characteristics of an effective soldier call for knowing what internal weapons and external weapons are needed in warfare. Internally, a soldier of any war must be disciplined to follow orders, which lead to the ultimate goal of a battle. Ability to be disciplined does not mean the absence of adaptability. Good soldiers know how to adjust quickly in a changing environment. War excels in chaos and turmoil. Successful soldiers are dependable; these individuals can be counted on to get the job done because they stay focused and persevere to the end. A good soldier knows that he cannot do it alone and operates as a team player. Unlike Lucifer, who lost his glory because he no longer wanted to be a team player adhering to the rules of engagement, a good soldier knows his position and fulfills the role of that position which includes respecting the roles of others. A soldier who succeeds demonstrates knowledge of the mission and terrain of the battle. Knowledge coupled with courage allows a person to maintain integrity, which leads to a character that's healthy spiritually, emotionally and mentally.

Certain pieces of mental equipment must be utilized to win a war. Winning must be an affair of the heart and the soul. There must be a training, readiness, and transforming in order to be combat capable. Effective training will result in having the strength, confidence and will to fit in and win anywhere at anytime. One must always be in the best mental shape to be called into duty at anytime. Transformation leads a good soldier to develop the ability to be agile, versatile and adaptive to changing circumstances.

As a soldier develops his inner resources, he must also make use of external sources. A soldier must wear protective gear, which will keep him from being an easy target. From his head to his feet, protection is needed. The head must be covered with a durable helmet to protect the control center. For the spiritual warfare, one must have settled in his mind the principles of the Creator and a will to stand on those principles in the worst of storms. A good soldier needs to have his feet and legs shod with appropriate footwear because there is no telling what mess he will step into. There must be the use of some shield like device to prevent the darts of the enemy from piercing the seat of his affections and other vital organs within. Like the weapon of prayer, the shield like device provides not only a defensive tool but also an offensive tool. It protects and wards off potential danger. Then there is the sword, which is often used as a tool of offense but can also be used to cut through thick brush and other obstacles placed in a soldier's pathway.

Another important piece of equipment is field communication. Prayer is not a tool of peacetime. Prayer is a walkie-talkie for the dangerous war-field not a small kitchen intercom for convenient household use. Because of the peace time use of prayer, many of us cannot experience the awesome potential of prayer. Thus, we open ourselves up for attack because we cannot ward off the clever enemies, which would prevent us from achieving the ultimate goal of battles— to receive in a fuller measure both the temporal and eternal glory! We must get beyond making life rosy with prayer by taking on the attitude that prayer is needed because while life is a bed of roses, those roses have pinching thorns. Our life is full of cherries, but the misuse of prayer as a peacetime weapon leads us to forget about the pits of the cherries. Prayer as a war time weapon, provides us with the ability to focus and lock into the target—the Word of God that shields us in sudden distress. It provides God's soldiers with the necessities to open the way through mine fields: to provide protection, to provide opportunities, a balm to heal wounded soldiers, to energize the weak soldiers and to call for reinforcements. Prayer is a necessity for war times. In times of peace, we should be enjoying the glory that has been bestowed upon us by returning thanks and giving praise.

The most powerful weapon, however, for a successful soldier is the willingness to die for the cause, to yield his will to his superior. A successful soldier who is well equipped and trained knows how to take a stand against evil and a stand for righteousness. This soldier is decisive and does not take a middle ground. When a soldier defects or wanders off into enemy territory as did the American, John Walker, who became a member of the Taliban, he or she is not fit for anything! When a good soldier makes use of the inner and outer equipment for warfare, he demonstrates clarity of purpose and conviction to win at all costs.

But what is the good soldier winning? A soldier in the greater war knows that the prize is the full glory of the Creator. The soldier wins the opportunity for the Creator to say of her/him as He did to Moses, "I speak face to face" (Exodus 33:11). To be in a face to face encounter with the LORD is to experience the full Shekinah glory. At this moment of existence and this phase of the GREAT WAR, we can only experience the glimmer of His glory, for we would not be able to withstand such an empowering brightness. Thus, the good soldier does not seek the good that was but reaches towards the better that is ahead! The effective soldier realizes that the GLORY of God is the spoil to be attained.

The measure of victory is the Glory of God. Both sides of the war are fighting for the glory of God but for different reasons. One wants to exalt His glory while the other desires to defame God's glory. What each of us must ask ourselves is what side of the war for Glory am I on? Whichever side you are on will determine if you will receive any glory or receive the full glory that He promises to those who not only have His principles sealed within but also endure until the end. There is no middle ground.

Arming For Warfare

Dressed in Heavenly armor, no foe can defeat
When we lay all our cares at the Master's feet,
For our Heavenly Father sits on His mercy seat;
Watching and listening to the tune of our beat.

If we raise up a standard in the power of His name
Pronouncing that our Victor has already came,
To dispel all our weakness our guilt and our shame;
He'll give us a crown for He will
forevermore be the same.

It's not by our own power or in our own might
That we'll win in this earthly
warfare—our spiritual fight,
But we must be sincere and shine forth our little light;
By holding on, standing firm and doing what is right.

Down through the ages, man's been
telling this gospel story,
And those that believe receive the
light of our Savior's glory,
And even though at times it seems
like a great mystery;
By arming for warfare, the faithful
has always won the victory.

When arming for warfare it's wise
to stand up with credence
Girding up the loins and going out on the offense,
And whenever the enemy attacks first,
just bring out the best defense;
Fighting in God's might, we'll feel
supernatural confidence.
©Aminga D. Burton-Bracy

To fight and win in a spiritual warfare, one has to have a thick skin; that positions him or her to fight and win. Fighting and winning calls for positioning oneself to receive greater glory. Every man, woman, boy and girl must be on guard at all times. God loves youth because they are strong. He is looking for strong men and women who are willing to stand up against all odds and position themselves to fight and win. No weak, sensitive, easily discouraged, one who is still searching to find oneself is positioned to receive greater glory. One that is well positioned has to be well balanced spiritually, mentally, emotionally and physically to be aligned with the Creator because whenever an adversary strikes, one must be ready to bear arms without looking around to see if he or she is positioned rightfully. My mom, Mrs. Velva Burton, says it best in the following poem she wrote for a youth program a few years ago.

Youth of God's Royal Army

Youth of God's royal army, peculiar, chosen, blest,
He calls in clarion tone, "stand up and pass the test."
Stand up youth's noble manhood,
and fight against the wrong;
You cannot fail! You must not fail!
Advent youth, be strong.

It is a blessing to be chosen at this crucial time,
When all around you are degradation, sin and crime.
God needs His chosen ones to hold His standard high,
And thus proclaim to all you meet,
"The Coming King is Nigh!"

As soldiers of the heavenly King,
you cannot shirk your task.
You dare not shift your challenge, nor for excuse ask.
So buckle now your armour on,
by studying God's word;
In frequent, fervent prayers, make
your petitions heard.

Too long you've been "standing at ease," gazing into space.
ATTENTION! ABOUT TURN! FORWARD MARCH!
Take your place,
At home, in the community, at
work, at school, or play,
In words and deeds preparing
souls, for the glorious day.
Velva Burton
© April 5, 1992

Chapter 7

WHAT TO EXPECT WHILE GOING THROUGH SUFFERINGS

When sufferings come, we temporarily lose our glory—a state of joy, peace, hope and harmony that come from oneness with our Creator; faith seems to go out through the back door as confusion and pain comes in through the front door. As humans, we tend to go through a shattered state of mind before we can deal with the glaring reality and truths staring us in the face. Thus, we easily enter a period of instant shock and panic. How long we remain in this state determines how and when our glory is shadowed. For example, when the Apostle Peter and his boys were on a ship sailing to the other side of the sea (Matthew 14 KJV) at Jesus' request, they encountered an unexpected storm. They immediately panicked not because of the raging winds and billowing waves rather at the sight of a being walking on water; a being they immediately took as a ghost. Their obvious fear of the unexpected and unknown coming towards them caused their glory, peace and harmony to flee from them until Jesus spoke assuredly, "Take courage! It is I. Don't be afraid" (Matt.14: 27 NIV).

But the real test in this event is Peter, for with all the confidence placed in this Miracle Worker, he desired to perform similar feats. He wanted, like Lucifer, to be Christ and to do what Christ could do. So, Peter asks Jesus if he could walk on the stormy lake to validate Jesus' identity. With assurance, Peter steps out. He walks toward Jesus. I can imagine that he got full of himself and showed off to the boy's back in the boat. As he turned to showcase his own endeavors on the water, Peter also took his eyes off of the LORD. Taking his eyes off of the LORD resulted in focusing his eyes on the stormy conditions. Immediately his feet disappeared, then his ankles, shins, knees and thighs all disappeared, too. Worse of all, his glory—peace and harmony with Jesus disappeared as the contrary conditions grew in appearance. Immediately, Peter panicked! The only thing he could do is that which we need to do more often in the midst of storms, he desperately cried out the simple phrase, "Lord, save me"!

When in the midst of the storm in the darkness of the day, we must be aware that the LORD's presence ever lingers waiting to envelop us. Like a ship on a thick, foggy night looking for a beacon of hope from the lighthouse, Jesus calls us to look up and over the horizon of the immediate impending doom that often comes our way. As we go through sufferings, we must realize that the experience provides opportunities through obstacles, promise through problems, healing power through hellish pain, and triumph through troubles. Though we go through sufferings, the only thing that remains is the blessings.

As preached by Dr. John Trusty, the unexpected contrary winds enter our lives for the following reasons:

1) Deepen our faith in the Creator
2) See how weak our strengths are and how strong our weaknesses are
3) Shake us out of our complacent state
4) Get us to be active
5) Take us where we would otherwise not go
6) Teach us how to pray
7) Make us wait on the LORD [1]

When we grow through sufferings, remaining focused on the glory of the Creator enables us to be eventual victors rather than eternal victims. Not everyone is strong enough to deal with the complexities and realities that suffering brings. Regardless of how high our esteem may be, we must expect that our confidence may be shaken during tough times. When tragedies strike, we become more vulnerable than usual, causing us to experience a wide range of explosive emotions like shock, anger, hate, despair, grief, agony, distress, sadness and fear. These are all normal emotions to feel in times of crisis, but it is unhealthy to feed them for too long! They can backfire and have adverse affects on our spiritual, mental, emotional, physical and social well being. Amid intense emotions we must allow ourselves time to grieve and heal.

When we give ourselves a chance to heal, we will be restored back to normalcy—better than normalcy, quicker and can overcome the adversity positively. Within each of us resides a supernatural ability to heal ourselves, but we cannot tap into it without tapping into Him who is the source and sustainer of this empowerment. Healing begins with prayerfulness then continues as we allow ourselves a chance to grieve. It culminates when we encourage and help restore others. Even in adverse times, we must not hesitate to do something good for someone else even if it entails forgiving those who have done us wrong. It is impossible to find healing if we are vindictively hurting others. While seeking healing through yielding to the Great Physician and serving those who may have brought on the dis-ease, we will become vulnerable. This vulnerability does not have to be a weakness; it can serve as the necessary point from which we rebound and climb to higher heights.

Most of us have been brought to our knees in the aftermath of the "Attack on America" not in surrendering to our adversaries but in submission to the will of God. So, as we elevate other elements of healing, we must bear in mind that the best way to overcome tragedy is to give ourselves time to grieve over our losses. Many of us may not have lost loved ones in the tragedy, but we all have lost something: homeland security, revenues, pride, home and more. Regardless of what we've lost, there is a good reason why we are grieving and the symptoms are the same. Thus, we need to find relief. Each stage of the grieving process is essential to the restoration process.

A Personalized 10-Step Process to Recover From Grief

To get through a difficult situation one has to learn what is a normal reaction and allow oneself the chance—challenging oneself to go through each of these stages that are critical to recovery. It must be understood that no two people are alike and even identical twins are different in how they react emotionally and physiologically. Therefore, while some may have special innate personality traits and spiritual gifts that allow them to skip over certain stage(s), others may have to go through particular phases longer than others do. The bottom line is doing what is necessary to get yourself through the process successfully, so you do not have to live with antagonism that keeps you repeatedly living through painful situations that are not properly dealt with.

There are four primary stages of grief recovery that we all must go through to deal with our painful ordeals healthily: *Denial*, *Anger*, *Despair* and *Acceptance*. Although everyone is different, most of us need a more in depth sequel of resolution to recover from a painful situation. Keep in mind that a loss is a loss regardless of the nature or extent, and it would be wise to seek closure on every painful circumstance you go through. Based on personal experience, I discovered a technique to get through difficulties in my life that helps me to fully recover. By combining the standard 4 processes (*Denial*, *Anger*, *Despair* and *Acceptance)* I learned in a grief recover seminar and psychology coupled with some personal experiences the following module. As we are confronted with painful situations, here are the ten steps we can expect:

1. **Shock** is usually the first thing one experiences when danger arises. In simple terms, shock is merely a numbness one feels that precedes a state of disbelief. It is what we experience when something unusual or unexpected happens in our lives making it difficult for us to fathom the reality of a painful situation. It has numbing effects on our physical, emotional and psychological well being. Although it is quite normal, it is imperative that we get through this state quickly to continue the healing process and avoid becoming fixated in this state.

2. **Panic** is another initial response that precedes the denial stage. As shock begins to wear off, panic (a sense of confusion) tends to set in. At this stage, one begins to come to a sense of awareness that something bad has just happened. Panic creates a feeling of sudden terror. It sends a person into a state of confusion not knowing what to do next, where to turn for help or how to approach the dreadful situation. Because an individual doesn't think logically during this time, he is likely to hurt himself or others unnecessarily. However dangerous this state may seem, it creates a sense of alertness that is necessary to prepare one for what psychologists call "fight or flight" when there is a clear and present danger.

3. **Denial** is actually the first major stage of the grieving process. After getting over the numbness and confusion, denial sets in. In this stage, one experiences disbelief about the ordeal and becomes aware that something drastic has happened. During

this stage a person begins to question or second-guess herself as to whether or not the ordeal really occurred. During this period of denial, there are physical manifestations of what is denied psychologically; some of which include loss of appetite, disturbance of normal sleep patterns and chronic fatigue. Loss of appetite can result in sudden and substantial weight loss. Disturbance of sleep can be getting too much or too little sleep. Signs of chronic fatigue are most visible when one is constantly tired, burned out or has low energy levels. One cannot become fixated in this stage for too long and remain normal. To become fixated in this phase leads to a more intense form of deception, self-denial.

4. **Anger** is the second major step to grief recovery. It tends to intensify as the reality of a situation sets in. Intense feelings of disdain and disgust directed at the person(s) one thinks is responsible for the painful situation indicates that he or she is in the anger stage. Excessive feelings of anger, violent outbursts or a sense of retaliation are all expected in this stage. The initial anger that is directed at the individual(s) viewed as the source of the suffering, if not controlled, can lead to hate or resentment that ultimately leads to regrets once truths are revealed. Publilius Syrus said that, *"An angry man is again angry at himself when he returns to reason."* When people are angry, they tend to close out logical reasoning—closing their minds and eyes to realities but always open their mouths. Robert Green Ingersoll asserts, *"Anger blows out*

the lamp of the mind." There needs to be a cooling-off period before responding to a crisis or those involved in a painful situation to prevent regretful decision. If taken in the right stride, anger begins with foolishness but ends with full repentance. This brings a person one step closer to closure, a rational resolution and healing.

5. **Despair** is the third major stage of grief recovery. It is at this stage that a person feels most hurt, fearful, helpless and hopeless. This is the stage where one begins to come to grips with his or her loss or adversity and can fully examine the extent of the damage done. Despair is often accompanied by intense feelings of unhappiness and overwhelming sadness. It is wondering if the bad situation will ever end. This is a miserable state of mind to be in because a person desires few things and has so many fears. The problems we face in life are not really the problem rather they are a manifestation of a greater, usually unseen, problem. When we expect things to be based on that which we obviously perceive, we discover other complications; we cannot overcome the surface problem without addressing the deeper problem. We want to deal with remote causes rather than the immediate cause for a problem. We must never forget that we may also find meaning in life even when confronted with a hopeless situation, when facing a fate that cannot be changed. For what then matters is bearing witness to the unique human potential at its best, which is to transform a personal tragedy into a triumph, to turn one's predicament into a human achievement (Viktor E. Frank, *Man's*

Search For Meaning). As hopelessness sets in, it leads to feelings of helplessness. When one feels hopeless, he may begin to wish he didn't exist. As miserable as one can be in this stage, it is one of the most important stages in the grieving process because, according to Annie Sophie Swetchine, *"The fact that God has prohibited despair gives misfortune the right to hope all things, and leaves hope free to dare all things."* Those who cheat this stage—skipping from the anger to another stage or choose to remain fixated in the anger stage often find themselves depressed. For those who allow themselves to go through this process, seeing it as a passing through stage where they can finally come to the reality, there is great hope for a bright and normal future.

6. **Acceptance** is the final scientific stage of grief recovery. When one welcomes the notion that he believes the circumstance is what it is rather than what he wants it to be or believes it to be, rest assured that he has made it to the acceptance stage of grief recovery. Acceptance is admitting that the problem exists in reality or that one has a problem and turns inward to look for plausible solutions. As a result, self-pity and skepticism will disappear because he has learned how to work out more acceptable behaviors. Accepting the situation for what it is makes a person see things for what they really are. Only until then can the confusion of suffering begin to clear up.

7. **Withdrawal** is not an "official" stage of the grief recovery process, but it is necessary to understand the intricate part it plays in the process, positively or negatively, to retain normalcy. During the withdrawal stage, a person is capable of detaching from a painful situation. The intense pain or agony she goes through makes her feel like no one else understands. This causes one to distance oneself from those who care and hide negative emotions rather than venting them. However, there is a more positive side to withdrawal. It can help her remove herself from the painful situation temporarily to find a positive place of escape. Some people need a little quiet time to ponder the painful events that just took place and time to figure out how to get move beyond them. Sometimes to recover, it may call for shutting off the television or whatever medium that bares bad news, if it is one of those situations that keeps the events playing back over and over like a recorder, triggering painful feelings. Then there are other times when it is necessary to go away, retire or recede from the reality in order to come to grips with oneself to gain strength and give oneself time to heal.

8. **Guilt** is normal though it is not listed as one of the main stages of recovery. The guilt stage is almost always present in grief recovery. As one heals, she may feel like there was something she could have done to change the outcome or change another's fate. People always feel as if they have let down or offended others if they get out of or through a painful situation that someone else did not make

it through. Because the guilt weighs so heavily on their shoulders, survivors often wish they could have traded places with another that was not so lucky. They often feel unworthy of surviving or guilty that they didn't save another. Cicero said, *"The greatest incitement to guilt is the hope of sinning with impunity."* Indeed one is only human that is haunted by the guilt of what she did or could not do. William Wordsworth said, *"From the body of one guilty deed a thousand ghostly fears and haunting thoughts proceed."* Guilt often leads to suspicion, which always seems to haunt a guilty mind. To move beyond guilt, one must acknowledge that he or she has the right to feel guilty and accept forgiveness for not being able to do more.

9. **Discomfort** is always felt where hurt and pain are found. The discomfort stage results from carrying guilty feelings around for a period of time. This is a stage where people feel uneasy in the presence of others or a situation they perceive as threatening. In this stage, everybody becomes a suspect because distrust often infiltrates the mind of an uneasy person. Oftentimes, those that feel uneasy make others feel uncomfortable. Discomfort can be a positive when it brings awareness that leads to finding credible solutions. Moving beyond the discomfort requires self-forgiveness and walking in the reality of that forgiveness. Nothing soothes the soul like a repentant heart. True confession eases discomfort and gives a positive outlet.

10. **Finding Viable Outlets** is the final stage that constitutes going through the recovery process to gain a positive resolution. Outlets are necessary channels to vent painful emotions. It's a progressive channel that influences the grief recovery progress, much like a light at the end of the tunnel. Here we can find constructive ways to redirect the pain we feel to find viable alternative solutions, probable ways of escape to vent painful emotions. This stage involves people reflecting back on a bad situations to see how fortunate they were to have gotten through the ordeal and then look for ways to rid themselves of the agony of the painful situation. Positive outlets include talking, writing, exercising, having a little fun, joining support groups, seeking expert help or finding ways to help others.

Some people can easily bounce back off the wall and heal individually—drawing strength from their inner spirits but not everyone is so fortunate. Many cannot positively tap into a defense mechanism that allows internal strengths to kick in quickly. Use of a defense mechanism is one of the strategies Freud posed that can help us prevent or reduce anxiety. Doing or thinking of doing something forbidden makes us anxious, but we can use our defense mechanism to express the impulse in disguise to avoid punishment by society or condemnation by the superego, thereby reducing the anxiety.[2] To find a positive outlet, our defense mechanism must not be used mal-adaptively, to deceive others, but in retrospection. That means replace negative attitudes, energies, feelings, ideas and thoughts by utilizing internal strengths—those positive attributes inside to overcome or get us out of bad situations.

We must find positive outlets to help us deal with or overcome painful situations. This may require a visit to a professional counselor, a psychologist or a clergy to help work through painful situations that may lead to maladaptive behaviors. We need alternatives to find a break through. Being in touch with our inner selves, strengths and weaknesses, which is critical to how successful we are in recovering. It's crucial to find out what works best for us individually and do it. Never worry about what others do and don't try to patronize them because what works best for them may not even work for you. Just be the best that you can be.

"Whatever You Are"

If you can't be a pine on top of the hill,
Be a scrub in the valley, but be
The best little scrub by the side of the rill;
Be a bush if you can't be a tree!
If you can't be a bush be a bit of the grass,
And some highway happier make,
If you can't be a muskie then just be a bass—
But the liveliest bass in the lake!
We can't all be captains, there's got to be crew,
There's something for all of us here,
There's big work to do, and there's lesser to do,
And the task you must do is the near.
If you can't be a highway then just be a trail,
If you can't be the sun be a star;
It isn't by size that you win or you fail—
Be the best of whatever you are!
Author Unknown

No two persons resolve the same problems exactly the same way; the way people handle problems vary. But prayer serves as a viable outlet that gives a solace knowing that there's someone bigger than our problems. Many testify that it helps to subdue some of their greatest fears. On the other hand, tears are involuntary actions; they have a way of coming naturally. They are not easily controlled when one has unexpressed emotions for tears are resourceful outlets. Writing is an effective outlet to vent pain; much relief is gained when painful situations are captured in some way on paper. Talking to others is one of the most valuable and inexpensive ways of venting pain, frustration and fears. Additionally, any physical activity is good for resolving painful experiences. It gives the body muscles that tend to tense up under duress a means of escape to relax. A positive outlet can be a person's ticket to healing and restoration, which is the essence of reaching for greater glory.

If you feel like the walls around are closing in on you or like the world around is about to fall apart then you probably have not found a viable outlet that will bring resolve. Despite the loss, misery and the strife that Satan has inflicted, God specializes in fixing the impossible and can help you to regain your composure, so you can find peace within. Losing someone that you love dearly or something that can't be easily replaced brings a sense of being overwhelmed by feelings of dis-ease and dis-comfort. The answer that you are looking for lies right within God's word. In the midst of the hurt and the pain you have to put your trust in God, for He alone can bring comfort and a shelter in the time of storms. At times, it seems like there is nothing but chaos in life, but God can turn things around if you rely totally on Him. In the midst of all our troubles, fears and strife God is working things out for you if you can hold out. You have to start right now by communicating with Him. Prayer is the single most important outlet that one will ever find because God can fill those lonely, empty feelings to give joy, peace and happiness inside. Mark Twain seemingly knew what adversity was about when he said, *"Grief can take care of itself: but to get the full value of joy you must have somebody to divide it with."* Even if no one is available to help as you face adversity, know that God is always near waiting to answer prays and bring back the glory if you'll rise up and reach out and get it. Here's a poem I wrote with you in mind to help you find positive outlets and encourage you to reach out so that you can access the power of God in your life.

Make a Positive Change
If you feel as if the wall
Around you, is about to fall,
Or like the world around may fall apart;
When loss, misery and strife won't depart.

Just start a revolution
Begin to make a resolution,
To get rid of the pollution;
You must be a part of the solution.

Find viable outlets that brings positive resolve
And all your problems may suddenly dissolve,
Around the lost or past, the world does not revolve;
For a great power that lies within
you quickly will evolve.

With God at hand to bless and guide
Deep love no adversity can ever hide,
For in His hands you safely abide;
No matter whatever may betide.

If you keep God always by your side
He'll walk ever close beside,
For within your heart he'll reside,
Filling lonely, empty feelings to
give joy and peace inside.
© Aminga Deana Burton-Bracy

Chapter 8

THINGS THAT SHRINK THE REACH TOWARDS FULL GLORY

All bad or negative actions, attitudes, attributes, deeds, habits and thoughts are things that shrink our reach towards full glory. These are maladaptive behaviors that must be changed if we are to be positioned to receive full glory. Maladaptive behaviors are detriments that block our prospect of living happy and productive lives. They rob us of some of life's greatest joys. When we do things that go against our voice of reasoning and our inner spirit tells us they are forbidden, we become anxious and stressed. Fear is one of the first maladaptive behaviors to which human beings adapted. Adam and Eve had to fight this fear demon as soon as they sinned. They feared and hid. They feared, and each blamed another for her and his choice. Fear impacts on our emotional, mental, social, physiological well being and is the underlying factor behind all other problems.

Regardless of what the situation may be, by committing forbidden acts, we shut out God's glory from our lives and begin to feel guilt, shame and discomfort. These feelings lead to deception: lies, running, hiding and fronting. It's easy to deceive man, but it is impossible to conceal things from our Creator. We may try to lie, run or hide from our Creator, but it will do us no good and will make His glory become inaccessible to us. Being in a position of fear causes us to become victim to one of the following three syndromes that are associated with Eve and Adam: Evitis, Adamitis, or AdamEvitis.

- **EVITES** are those who take to one of the following maladaptive behaviors.
  - (1) Wander away from paths of righteousness until they end up on enemy territory.
  - (2) Become lured by the snakes: evil communication, popular opinion, greed, pride, lust, peer pressures, cheating and deception.
  - (3) Easily persuaded by others to change their values, opinions and beliefs.
  - (4) Unsure what one stands for and easily falls for anything.
  - (5) Find reason and excuses to cover wrong doings.

- **ADAMITES** are those people who find themselves:
  - 1) Beginning to wander away from paths of righteousness into an enemy's camp.
  - 2) Enjoying running or hiding behind others: walk in the shadows of others or lose their identity because they have taken on so many others that's not ideally theirs.
  - 3) Exhibiting co-dependent behaviors: relies on others, substances, clothes or group for their feelings of self worth.

4) Compromising values in exchange for love, sex, money, recognition, power.

5) Blaming others for their problems or cynical feelings.

6) Buying into another's skepticism without proving all things.

- **ADAMEVITES**—These are people that commit forbidden acts and rather than facing the repercussions and learning from the situation.

    1) They specialize in running and hiding to mask their true identity, their shortcomings and their weaknesses.

    2) They alienate themselves from those they love most because of the suspicions and secrets they don't want uncovered.

People that run or hide rob themselves of glory; the farther they wander into the forest of gloom and despair the harder it is to stop masking. Such an attitude leads one to feel misery, guilt and shame. This causes people to lose not only temporal glory but also eternal glory. Such maladaptive behaviors may hinder them from turning their lives around, giving up the chance to go back into the Garden that was lost to our fore-parents.

Satan is the master deceiver; if we are not careful, we may play into his territory and lose our glory. When we take on anyone of the above symptoms, we are unable to grow in ways that are crucial to bask in the sunshine of God's love; we become stagnated and irritable. According to Murphy's Law, "Almost anything is easier to get into than out of." Those actions, attitudes and characteristics that we formulate as a result of insisting to do things that we know are forbidden, not acceptable by society or our Creator, leads to more dangerous behaviors that can affect our overall well being. Maladaptive behaviors are things we harbor in our lives that we try to push under the rug or pretend that they either don't exist or try to convince ourselves that they are okay when they are not. They prevent us from living optimal lives.

The key to avoid collecting maladaptive behaviors is not yielding to temptation or giving in to enticements, those things the inner spirit signifies are wrong. We also would do well to shun evil companions while listening to the voice of reason inside. If we have already yielded to the imprisoning behaviors then we do not need to stop justifying those behaviors but try to correct them as soon as the act is committed. The longer we allow them to continue, the more intense the urge will become to repeat them. As Murphy's law states, "The longer it takes for an error to be detected and corrected, the more likely it will turn out that it was correct in the first place." If we allow ourselves to form habits from constantly practicing maladaptive behaviors then more than likely we will become unstable. The only way to get help for such deviant behavior is to recognize and correct them instead of trying to justify them.

To fully understand how we develop maladaptive behaviors that tend to control us, we have to go back and look at Freud's personality structure where the id, the ego and the superego interact to govern our behavior. These three components of personality tend to oppose each other in functions, for the ego functions to postpone instant gratification that the id wants immediately and the super ego battles with both because our behavior often falls short of the moral code of conduct it represents. In people who have well-integrated personality structures, the ego remains in firm but flexible control as the reality principle governs. The ego tends to obey the reality principle, delaying the gratification of impulses until the opportune time presents itself.

A typical example of this rule is the sexual impulses that all of us possess. While well-integrated people who are confronted with things that arouse or stimulate them sexually do not readily jump to gratify those impulses, not so well integrated people do. Instead of making a spur of the moment decision to act on a sexual impulse, the ego of well integrated people often presents them with the reality that the time or place is not appropriate to act on that feeling. Think of what would happen in our society if we all acted on the sexual impulses to acquire the instant gratification that our id initiates? Well-adapted people have healthy sexual drives and are well integrated. They find appropriate ways to control their ego so that it does not respond to the advancements the id wants immediately. When the suitable time comes, hopefully with a spouse in privacy and intimacy, a well-balanced individual will become gratified in the most rewarding ways. That is the reality principle. Anyone who acts on his/her impulse to immediately satisfy himself/herself sexually or in any other way exhibits maladaptive behavior that leads to repercussions and lost glory— joy, peace and harmony.

To rise above maladaptive behaviors we have to reach for greater glory and channel the energy that causes us to want to act on an impulse inappropriately into more desirable ways. Both suppressing and repressing negative energies can become problematic. We have to learn how to recharge those negative energies in more positive outlets because those energies are inherent; therefore, they cannot be destroyed. All well-adjusted people know where their strengths and weaknesses lie and take advantage of opportunities to channel those negative behaviors in more desirable ways. This group of people also looks for threats—any thing that would hamper progress or block any prospects of growing in desirable ways because they understand that the energy they possess is normal and cannot be destroyed. It is wise to look not only for opportunities but also for threats because they are the *labido* (i.e., lust) that drives us to want to act out those initial desires we possess that are inherent in us.

We all can rise above those lustful desires and other maladaptive behaviors but not of our own selves. Humanly, we can express those impulses in a disguised form to avoid punishments by society, family, religion and friends or condemnation from the superego. Though that may reduce the anxiety momentarily, it is what leads us to form maladaptive behaviors in the first place. The only way to escape the undesirable sexual or emotional impulses that cause maladaptive behaviors is to channel them in more productive ways. Because we are born in sin and shaped in iniquity, we cannot escape until we begin reaching for greater glory, which calls for self-denial. God can help us rise above our present circumstances to regain our glory, which allows us to escape the feelings of lost glory—guilt, misery, shame and anger.

The Flip Side of Anger

Anger is one of the most detrimental of all our internally triggered emotions that if not used constructively can become a maladaptive behavior. The flip side of anger is sadness and loneliness. We become angry when sadness or loneliness are built up within because we hold on to old baggage from past painful experiences. Sadness is the underlying feeling we derive as a result of loss, lack or limitations. It tends to block off God's glory eventually from our lives if we do not learn to cope with the realities of the painful situations. When anger is not dealt with constructively, it leads us to develop resentment against others all because we choose to hang on to pain that is associated with the hurt that brings on sadness and loneliness. A heart that doesn't feel the need to let go of old baggage that brings on sadness chooses to stay in a dangerously destructive and unproductive state of mind. Take the admonition of Katrina North *"Let go of your worries and concerns. Just hand them over to God. Then simply focus your mind on God—his power, majesty and wisdom. Invest ten minutes in this practice daily, and you'll find serenity—even in the middle of the most frantic schedule."* Doing this, we can find triumph when through our anger we lose our temporal glory. We cannot hold on to anger, or it will destroy us.

Anger has the tendency to distort our perception of reality, destroy our self-image and diminish our spiritual progress, but we must not allow it. When angry feelings are coming on, we have to fight them with all of our spiritual energy because once this habit is formed, it is difficult to break. We should remember the adage, "an ounce of prevention is better than a pound of cure." The most important aspect of the recovery process that was mentioned previously, that brings us closure is the control of anger. Hanging on to past pain prohibits us from reaching out to the glory that lies ahead leaving us in a present state of frustration.

In the book of Proverbs, anger is referred to in a number of less than productive ways. Here's what some Biblical writers say about anger. Solomon said, *"Anger stirreth up strife,"* David said, *"Cease from anger, and forsake wrath: fret not thyself in any wise to do evil. For evildoers shall be cut off: but those who wait upon the Lord, they shall inherit the earth"(Psalm 37:8),* and James says in the first chapter of his epistle, *"Let every man be swift to hear, slow to speak, slow to wrath: for the wrath of man worketh not the righteousness of God"* (1:19). To relieve oneself of the excess baggage of anger is to position oneself to be restored. Those who are holding on to unresolved anger have to put it away, or it destroys the soul and the possibilities of reaching greater glory. One of the ways to block out anger from our lives is not to feed it. To block out anger, we have to turn our resentments into productive outlets and in times of struggle and conflict, let go and let God fix our problems for us. This can help us heal from the pain of anger that is derived from the sadness we feel as a result of lack, loss and limitations.

Regardless of whether someone did us wrong or not, who did what or who did not do what is unimportant in the sight of God. No amount of negative alliances or allies we accumulate through manipulation and distortion of the truth can give us joy, peace and harmony that comes from oneness with our Creator. Because our Creator is the author of LOVE, we are no exception to this rule. Unless we are covered with God's righteousness, we will not escape the abyss of dark despair that is associated with sadness and will have to continue running and hiding farther away from the reach of glory much like our fore-parents. It is easy to mask (run, hide or front) from each other, but it is impossible to run or hide from God no matter how deep into the forest we go. Irrespective of what any other person might say, we need the power of Christ to deliver us from this travesty that anger has landed us into. The only way out is to reach for greater glory starting with exhibiting love, forgiving those who do us wrong, rising above what is past and letting go so that God can begin putting things back into their perspective place.

Dangers of Masking Pain

Another major thing that shrinks our reach of fuller glory is masking; that is, running, hiding and fronting. Masking is a deceptive behavior that all of us assume at certain difficult times in our lives. While it may be appropriate on some temporary basis, if masking is not quickly corrected then it may produce severe consequences. Most people mask to cover up any inappropriate behavior while at the same time charade those behaviors they deem desirable. There are two main reasons why people mask undesirable behaviors. For one, they are afraid that society may look down on them if they think they are deviating from social or cultural norms. On the other hand, many people are scared to face their inner Spirit because they are aware that it may not condone certain behaviors and may convict them causing dis-ease. As innocent as these two reasons may appear, there is a real danger to mask undesirable behaviors for excessive periods of time. Excessive masking can have adverse affects on one's emotional, mental, spiritual and physiological well being.

Fear is the underlying factor of masking. Deep down within, we are aware of our imperfections, even ones that no one else but us can see. We fear that if others see the imperfections then we may not be accepted for who we really are. It is far more rewarding letting people know us the way we are even if it means that they can't identify with us and want to disassociate with us. If all of us can understand that we all have flaws then no matter how we look or feel there are strengths and weaknesses that are embedded in us. By being ourselves, others who are much like ourselves are drawn to us; thus, we will seemingly avoid less stress and conflicts; "birds of a feather flock together." Why try to pretend we are someone we're not when we can treasure those who accept us for who we really are without putting up with the drama of walking in another's shadow?

There was a time in my life when I tried to mask my fears, run from reality, hide from truths and front that I was some character I wasn't, but that didn't help me to get over my pain. Rather it intensified my pain and ate away at my self-esteem. Later on in life, I came to realize that there was no gain in deflecting a painful situation because it wouldn't help me overcome. It was difficult for me to break the cycle of masking but according to Murphy's law, "If you mess with a thing long enough, it will break." That law held true for me because after much determination, I managed to stop masking and now some do not like me, but there are many people who do love and affirm me just the way I am. Now, instead of trying to fit in, I just put a premium on those who value me for who and whose I truly am. At the same time, I keep working to improve my character continuously, not to seek the approval of others but in order to grow into the new me that God wants and expects of me.

Deceptive behaviors like masking cheat us of the learning and transformation process that overcoming brings as we reach for greater glory. The one true test of overcoming is to stay in the storm no matter how fierce it gets—facing our worst fears head on and confronting those undesirable behaviors by fixing them in a productive way. By listening to the voice of reasoning inside and using wisdom and understanding in all our affairs, we can fix anything about us with God's help. This can never happen as long as we try to act like another or walk in another's shadow. All masking is going to do for us is make us more co-dependent on another; thus, leaving us feeling more vulnerable and insecure. Satan knows our weaknesses; when we are susceptible to another, he will use that one to manipulate, use, victimize or traumatize us until we give up or lose hope. No matter how hard one tries there are two beings one can't mask to: our *Maker* and the *great deceiver*. Masking causes us to wander away from the path to the glory of God and makes us more susceptible to our enemies and the great deceiver, Satan, will hound us down for *"nature sides with the hidden flaw"* but *"the hidden flaw never remains hidden forever"* (Murphy's Law).

I find that in the storm, there are dark clouds, heavy hail, strong winds, high waves and raging tempests, but these are where we learn to face and conquer our fear, our weaknesses, our realities and our pain; this takes strength beyond our own. In the storm, we learn to look to the hills, the rock Christ Jesus, from which comes our help. When we find Christ as we go through the storm, we will be calmer because He assures us. One who runs from a unavoidable storm looks for the easy way out but what happens is that he has to keep facing that storm over and over again until he perfects those characteristics that Christ wants to transform. We must stay in the storm and rely on God to hide us from the pestilence.

Godly people have no need to run or hide, front or mask because by keeping our motives pure we will not wander off into the wilderness of guilt, shame and discomfort. Secrets are our silent killers; they eat away at our body, mind and soul. We have to understand that though we may get by with eluding our fellowmen with our secret faults we will never hide from God, *"for in Him we live, and move, and have our being..."* (Acts 17:28).

Our Heavenly Father is our Creator—the one that made us and He sees and knows what happens to or with us and nothing we do, think or say is hidden from Him. No matter how hard we try, even the most cunning and deceptive among us cannot run or hide from Him. However, despite our frailties, sinfulness, wickedness and straying from the paths of righteousness, He still loves us with an everlasting love and cares about the pain we experience while we are outside of the realms of His glory. Like Adam and Eve, we have to step from out of our hiding place so that God can soothe our troubled minds, for He has made provisions for us through His Son. Though it is impossible to elude the penalties of sin (death, guilt and shame) that we are all touched by one way or the other while living in this sinful world, we have a hope and the prospect of achieving greater glory. If we live humbly and walk circumspectly in God's sight, we can be reconciled back to Him through the Son that He has sent. Stepping out from behind the mask calls for a little bit more than is naturally required. The following poem helps us to see what it takes to step out from behind the mask.

Stepping Out From Behind the Mask

Behind the mask, there is unease and discomfort
But with right motives you can feel divine comfort,
For by expelling all the hurts and
doubt that's felt inside;
There's tranquility and serenity no
matter what ever betide.

Behind the mask, there are awful little secrets
Lies and deceit that comes nor
leaves without deep regrets,
And the only way to relieve such a troubled soul,
Is to confess and make finding
forgiveness a personal goal.

Behind the mask, we run or hide in terror and fear
But that doesn't have to be so if we use our inner gear,
For strength of inner spirit shields and bring peace;
And that comes when it is expected the least.

Behind the mask, there are heartaches and pain
Where there should be sunshine and rain,
Stepping out is filled with harmony, joy and peace;
For being true all contention and strife will cease.

Stepping out from behind the mask
Calls for loyalty and willingness to complete a task,
It takes rising above what is in the present or past;
Letting go of ills done, then standing
firm and holding fast.
©Aminga Burton-Bracy

Unless we take off the mask, stop running and hiding, quit fronting or stop lying, we will be led into self-deception and risk losing both temporal and ultimate glory. One who does not willingly let go of old baggage and throw out the garbage is not positioned so that God can come in and shine His light of love on that life, revealing His glory.

An Unforgiving Spirit

A third thing that shrinks our reach for fuller glory is an unforgiving spirit. Fostering an unforgiving spirit causes us to agonize over wrongs that others do unto us, so we refuse to let go of the pain that is associated with the hurtful situation. This causes us to defy truths, doubt the power of God and limit ourselves to what we are capable of in our own strength. When Peter asked Christ how many times he should forgive his brother when he sins against him, Jesus told him seventy times seven (Matthew 18:21-22). Christ likewise instructs us to rebuke one that sins against us; if he or she asks forgiveness, we must forgive (Luke 17:3-4). The Lord never requires concealing a wrong deed that was done against us, for He knows it would lead to deception. Similarly, Jesus sanctions *"love your enemies, do good, and lend, hoping for nothing in return; and your reward will be great, and ye will be sons of the Most High. For He is kind to the unthankful and evil. Therefore, be merciful, just as your Father is merciful"* (Luke 6:35-37). It does not get any plainer than this. The reason why forgiveness is crucial is that our Heavenly Father will forgive us (Matthew 6:14, 15).

Forgiveness not only frees the forgiver, but it releases the forgiven soul. Dr. Edith Eva Eger, a Holocaust survivor, sees the forgiveness process as, *"Not forgiving someone for what they did to you. It's you wanting to release the part in you that makes you feel hurt. I wanted to live a full life, I have been able to do that because I have always celebrated every moment of what is left."* At times the enemy does wrong against us, for He knows if he can get us to default the forgiveness process then he has a chance of reaping havoc on our lives. We have to understand that *"Forgiveness,"* according to Hannah *Arendt, "is the key to action and freedom."* Unless we forgive men of their trespass against us, our Heavenly Father will not forgive us, and there is no hope of a temporal glory or any prospect of future ultimate glory. The Archbishop Desmond Tutu substantiates this by saying, *"There is no future without forgiveness."*

A little while back I did a survey to test how forgiving I was; I was quite shocked; so many of us think of ourselves more highly than we really are. After taking that test, I went to work on myself—surprisingly, the same test came back up on the beliefnet.com website. After taking it again, I felt like it was worth it because it monitored my progress. It would probably not hurt if you, too, took the test to see how forgiving you really are and for your sake, be honest with yourself.

Q1. When someone cuts you off in traffic, do you:

- ❑ Tusk, but don't do anything.
- ❑ Tap your horn and mutter darkly to yourself.
- ❑ Lean on the horn, roll down your window, and shout.

Q2. You run into someone from high school who wasn't very nice to you.

- ❏ You greet them, but are reserved, and end the conversation soon.
- ❏ You ignore them.
- ❏ You greet them and smile. It's water under the bridge.

Q3. You and a friend make weekend plans. The friend cancels at the last minute.

- ❏ You express your annoyance and tell the friend you're going to be on your guard next time.
- ❏ You tell the friend it's fine, and look forward to rescheduling.
- ❏ You say it's fine, but don't call the friend for a while.

Q4. Two people cut in front of you at an ice cream shop. Later, you notice police about to ticket their car for a meter violation.

- ❏ You have plenty of quarters, but walk away from the car, whistling a jaunty tune.
- ❏ You have plenty of quarters and drop just one in the meter.
- ❏ They get 15 minutes, no more. You put two or three quarters in the meter. A ticket is a big deal, even for jerks.

Q5. A friendly neighbor hits your pet with his car. The pet will be OK, but is in pain for several weeks.

❏ You cut off all contact with the neighbor.
❏ You treat him as before.
❏ You stop chatting over the fence with him, but you still pick up his mail for him when he's on vacation.

Q6. A basically decent person who seriously wronged you at a previous job has an interview at your new company. The boss asks your opinion.

❏ You know that the person would do a good job, and say so.
❏ You say the person would do a good job, but mention that you had a few personal issues with him.
❏ You know he would do a good job, but tell the boss not to hire him.

Give yourself a score. For example, if your response to question 1 is 1, score yourself a 10; if your response to question 1 is 2, give yourself a score of 6 and if your answer to question 1 is 3, score yourself a 3. When finished, tabulate a total of your score then refer to the notes below to evaluate how forgiving you are.

Question 1	
1.	10
2.	6
3.	3
Question 2	
1.	6
2.	3
3.	10
Question 3	
1.	6
2.	10
3.	3
Question 4	
1.	3
2.	6
3.	10
Question 5	
1.	3
2.	10
3.	6
Question 6	
1.	10
2.	6
3.	3
TOTAL	

You scored the total you tabulated, on a scale of 0 to 60. Here's how to interpret your score:

- 0 - 20 **Revenge**. Though a thirst for justice can be admirable, your insistence on an 'eye for an eye' may be poisoning your relationships with others. Next time you have a chance to retaliate let it pass.

* 21 - 40 **A balanced forgiver**. You're a basically kind person with a sense of balance and boundaries. However, you're no Mother Theresa.

* 41 - 60 **Very merciful.** Some people would call you a sucker, and some religions would call you a 'Holy Fool.' You're so merciful you may surprise others.

To let go of things that shrink our reach of greater glory, we have to allow the love of Christ to constrain us. A wise person wrote the following to his or her friends, a message applicable to all of those who are holding on to a maladaptive behavior that is shrinking the reach of greater glory. It said, "To all my friends who are:"

MARRIED
Love is not about "it's your fault", but "I'm sorry", not "where are you 'but "I'm right here", not "how could you" but "I understand", not "I wish you were", but "I'm thankful you are."

ENGAGED
The true measure of compatibility is not the years spent together but how good you are for each other.

NOT SO SINGLE
Love isn't about becoming somebody else's "perfect person." It's about finding someone who helps you become the best person you can be.

HEARTBROKEN

Heartbreaks last as long as you want and cut deep as you allow them to go. The challenge is not how to survive heartbreaks but to learn from them. Heartbreaks last as long as you want and cut deep as you allow them to go. The challenge is not how to survive heartbreaks but to learn from them.

NAÏVE

How to be in love: Fall but don't stumble, be consistent but not too persistent, share and never be unfair, understand and try not to demand, and get hurt but never keep the pain.

SEARCHING

True love cannot be found where it does not truly exist, nor can it be hidden where it truly does. Love is magic. The more we hide it, the more it shows; the more you suppress it, the more it grows.

PLAYBOY/GIRL TYPE

Never say I love if you don't care. Never talk about feelings if they aren't there. Never touch a life if you mean to break a heart. Never look in the eye when what you do is lie. The cruelest thing a guy can do to a girl is to let her fall in love when he doesn't intend to catch her fall.

POSSESSIVE

It breaks your heart to see the one you love happy with someone else but it's more painful to know that the one you love is unhappy with you.

AFRAID TO CONFESS

Love hurts when you break up with someone. It hurts even more when someone breaks up with you.

But love hurts the most when the person you love has no idea how you feel.

STILL HOLDING ON
A sad thing about life is that when you meet someone who means a lot to you, only to find out in the end that it was never bound to be and we just have to let go.

SINGLE
Love is like a butterfly. The more you chase it, the more it eludes you. But if you just let it fly, it would come to you when you least expect it. Love can make you happy but often times it hurts, but love's only special when you give it to someone who is worth it. So take your time and choose the best!

"Love is patient; love is kind... It bears all things, believes all things, hopes all things, endures all things" 1 Corinthians 13:4,7

By reaching out in love, we derive freedom from destructiveness of anger, masking and an unforgiving spirit, for God will restore us back to a healthy normal mindset; one that opens up to Him and is conducive for the kind of growth that causes us to attain glory. It is when we are at our lowest ebb that we need to reach out to our Heavenly Father because that is when He can access us most, when we step outside of our imperfect selves and allow Him to go to work on our weaknesses. It's time to let go of anything that makes us want to run or hide from our fellowmen and our Maker, Deliverer, Savior and King.

Chapter 9

THINGS THAT EXTENDS THE REACH TOWARDS GREATER GLORY

The things that extend one's reach towards full glory are the very things that draw us away from self-destruction and those adverse things around us. Becoming too wrapped up in ourselves and those people or things around us makes it impossible for us to reach beyond the boundaries of our earthly struggles because we often become sidetracked and consumed by panic or worry. But why worry when by positioning ourselves to extend our reach, we can have all the blessings of the moment. According to Corrie ten Boon, *"Worrying is carrying tomorrow's load with today's strength— carrying two days at once. It is moving into tomorrow ahead of time. Worry does not empty tomorrow of its sorrow, it empties today of its strength*[1].*"* We are also limited to the reach of glory when we become self-absorbed; that causes us to become fruitless and unproductive in our social, economic and spiritual lives.

To get to the top and at the same time feel hopeful, joyful, peaceful, and be in harmony with God and man, one has to position oneself to extend the reach towards fuller glory. Positioning oneself increases the reach towards greater glory, but it has nothing to do with conquering and/or dividing the spoils. Too many people think that to position oneself requires toppling someone else, as in the king or queen of the mountain syndrome. The effective reach towards fuller glory requires pulling others up with us as we extend our reach. Trampling on others may seem like the popular or right thing to do, and perhaps at times may seem like the quick way to get ahead; however, it is never lasting, for it neither positions us to remain at the top nor extends our reach to fuller glory. When our human nature shouts the things to do, Solomon reminds us in Proverbs 14:12, *"There is a way that seemeth right unto a man but the end thereof are the ways of death."* Those who align themselves with the Creator, do things that increase their reach towards greater glory. To position oneself, one has to practice the following basic A, B, C's:

I. Acknowledge faults and failures,
II. Become sensitive to the needs of others,
III. Confess faults one to another,
IV. Deny self and restore the one who has been hurt back to his or her rightful mind,
V. Examine self—re-evaluate self to see if there's any wicked way within and then,
VI. Forgive those who have trespassed or ask forgiveness of those one has trespassed.

Positioning oneself involves stepping out of the norm—the comfort zone. To do this, we place ourselves in a position to have our scope broadened: that means improving our relationship with our Creator, our relationship with others and a fuller understanding of ourselves. Broadening one's scope to receive greater glory, is to practice the **J.O.Y.** formula: <u>J</u>esus first, <u>O</u>thers second, and <u>Y</u>ourself last. One must be properly aligned to experience real JOY; otherwise, one will have to spend time allowing the Creator to work on him or her first. How else could one love the Father and others without first being able to love him/herself? To do that, one must master a few things: exercise forgiveness, have unconditional love, rise above what is past, practice peacemaking, hold daily devotion, be optimistic, and increase in wisdom and understanding.

1. **Exercising Forgiveness**

   Exercising forgiveness is a key component that increases one's reach towards greater glory. Forgiveness is the controlling of one's emotion by letting go of past, willful or accidental, injuries and rising above the hurt or pain inflicted by another. It takes will power and strength of inner spirit to position oneself to give or receive forgiveness.

   To position oneself to receive or give forgiveness, one has to endure hardships: critique, criticism, suffering, scorn or ill intent that another imposes. However, many who claim to be religious and highly spiritual or consider themselves Christians are still having difficulty with the issue of forgiveness. It is difficult enough to forgive ourselves after transgressing because of the brokenness of spirit that we feel with the consciousness of sin, but forgiving someone who has done us wrong is more difficult. The awareness of being trespassed against or trespassing on others compels those who are rightfully positioned to seek and give forgiveness.

Forgiveness granted or received enables us to access fuller glory because we allow the following to take place.

I.   Letting go of old baggage and letting God have His full way
II.   Acknowledging faults and weaknesses without looking for excuses.
III.   Allowing God to grant us the courage to change things deserving of a change.
IV.   Accepting that it's not possible to change others.
V.   Embracing others differences helps us see that we aren't so perfect ourselves.
VI.   Rising above what is past, leaving cares behind to receive the blessings of the moment.
VII.   Being free, for it takes God's forgiveness to free us from our burdens that keeps us bound and helps us live happier lives.

2. Having Unconditional Love

Having unconditional love for God and man is a key component of increasing our reach towards fuller glory. It positions us to exhibit faith. The entire basis of one's faith is built upon this very principle. When we love others, we are to love them regardless of what they do or how they act. Unconditional love is not based on our perspective but on faith.

God loves us with an everlasting love, unconditionally, and all He requires from us is that we return the full favor to Him and our fellowmen. Regardless of what we do, God doesn't stop loving us; there are no conditions, so why place conditions on our love for each other. At times, as human beings we can be quite selfish. We want others to love us irrespective of our imperfections; yet, we often limit the way we love others. Placing conditions on the way we love is not love; it's selective and shrinks our reach. To be positioned to receive full glory, we have to dismantle the conditions we place on others and begin to love unconditionally.

Whenever conditions are placed upon love, it removes the measure of faith that the Christian principle is built upon and causes defilement. Love and faith go hand in hand. It is difficult to love one that doesn't love us back in the same manner, one who trespassed against us, one who wrongfully accused us, one who despitefully misused us and one who causes us pain; however, we exhibit faith when we love anyway. Forgiving one that refuses to let go of our past mistakes is also an indication that we are positioning ourselves to give unconditional love and that increases our reach towards greater glory.

We can't sit around like hypocrites hating those who use extreme measures to condemn or convict others about their belief when everyday our lack of love results in fruitlessness that causes many souls to be lost spiritually or physically. Often times, we look down on and despise people who use extreme measures to enforce their beliefs and of course there should be great concern. However, the way we address our concern and how we treat each other kill far more people than the terrorist, vigilante and the legalist. More people die each day from stress related and psychological problems that are triggered by others than are killed by one of those extreme groups in one instance. Those who haven't noticed should take a good look around at the rate of deaths caused by suicide; depressions; heart attacks; violence that are triggered by hatred, envy or scorn etc. The subtleties of conditional love are as destructive to humanity as extreme measures because they have equally devastating effects on lives.

When we love someone unconditionally, we want to spend as much time in that person's presence as is possible. So, we embrace their difference, value their company and tolerate their shortcomings. However, many of us fall short of that mark. Instead of extending our reach towards greater glory, we diminish it and miss out on the benefits of unconditional love because we become so self-absorbed that we do things based on condition. Although we were taught in our homes and the church of God's love, we fail to practice this fundamental law actively. We may sing of love, talk of love, teach of love and pray for love but when the ultimate test comes, we fail because of our lack of tolerance for each other's differences and this is not exclusive to culture, sex and race. Still, we talk so much about going to heaven.

The question is "How can we love one another forever, if we can't love one another today?" Unconditional love is loving others the way God loves us despite our faults and sins. Just as God looks beyond our faults and sees our needs; likewise, we too must do this for our fellowmen.

God never asked us to love people that act like us, talk like us or think like us; neither those people who love us back, for He has a very different concept of love. Here is a visual of what God wants and expects of us if we are to receive His divine glory.

- Love those who do us wrong
- Love our enemies
- Be accountable for our Christian brothers and sister
- Reach out to the poor and homeless
- Love our neighbors
- Witness to the lost
- Reconcile our differences
- Share with those who have less

The Bible tells us that "Love is of God and everyone that loveth is born of God and knoweth God. He that loves not, knoweth not God for God is love." There is no such thing as conditional love; one can either love unconditionally or be hateful. 1 Corinthians 13 is the epicenter of love principles in the Bible. If our lives do not reflect such unconditional love, perhaps it's time to begin positioning ourselves and reach for it. By positioning oneself, one can extend the reach and reap the fruits of his or her labor because when God plants unconditional love in a heart, it will grow. In turn. It will come back to bless that one.

Glorious living doesn't exist without unconditional love—being in harmony with God and man. Harmony constitutes tolerating each other, getting along with others, reconciling our differences, giving and receiving forgiveness and sharing our faith. When we love people, we do not want to see them hurt in any way. That means, going out of the way to help them escape the things that shrink the reach towards greater glory. Unconditional love has both intrinsic and extrinsic rewards as well as positions us to expand our reach for greater glory.

3. Rising Above What Is Past

Rising above what is past increases our reach towards greater glory; it elevates us to deny selfish desires, resist temptation and overlook problems when our human nature tries to dominate our thought process and dictate our actions. Many believe that rising above what is past is pride, self-exaltation and self-absorption but they are wrong. None of those three has anything to do with rising. Rising above what is past is allowing God's empowering arms to lift a drooping spirit above everyday problems, unexpected storms and pain; then bring peace, joy, hope and harmony into that life.

To position oneself for greater glory, one has to first search one's soul for anything that is unlike Christ (past mistakes, sins, adversities, unforgiveness, failures, over indulgence and wrongs that were done to or against someone). None of us are perfect, for all like sheep have strayed from the paths of righteousness—away from a place where God's divine presence is felt.

That's why we have to position ourselves for the rise. No matter how hard we try, it is impossible to do it in our own strength; we must rely on God to elevate us, rising can position us for greater glory.

In this world, we are all sufferers and positioning ourselves to rise above what is past is not always easy. Sometimes it may mean that we have to risk standing up for what is right in the face of ridicule, criticism and scorn, but the payoffs are far greater. It may not be possible for humanity to grow wings, but we can take rising lessons from birds and allow God to lift our drooping spirits high above our present and past problems, hurt or pain. People who reach, position themselves to rise above every difficulty like fear, limitations, grudges, adversities, ignorance, arrogance and prejudices of the past. This can be done by reaching out and tapping into our highest source of power. Like Victor Hugo states so cleverly, we must:

"Be Like the Bird
That, pausing in her flight
A while on boughs too slight,
Feels them give way
Beneath her and yet sings,
Knowing that she hath wings."

Again, soaring like birds may not be humanly logical but it's not impossible with God's empowering, for He can elevate our minds to rise above anything. Those who study the life of birds are aware that some bird-like characteristics may help humanity escape the pains, temptations, disappointments, stress, problems and consequences that life brings everyday.

Take for instance the geese flying in a "V" formation. Scientific explanation poses that when each bird flaps its wings, it creates a revival for the other birds that follow closely behind. As human beings, these lessons are pertinent for our survival. God's sheltering wings revive those who follow closely in His footsteps. The updraft of the spirits of those who are inclining, in turn propels others upwards. Even after a hard fall, God's updraft propels us back upwards, so we can get up again quickly without holding a grudge or feeling guilt.

Troubles may pull us downwards, but we don't have to stay down if we keep positioning ourselves to rise above them regardless how bad it may seem at the time. Only those who allow God's Spirit to elevate them can rise above what is past and position themselves for greater glory. In positioning myself and allowing the updrafts of God's spirit to lift me above my past difficulties, I can affirm Washington Irving's saying, "Little minds are tamed and subdued by misfortune; but great minds rise above them." Elevation from the updraft of God's spirit helps me to elevate others, and I neither become tamed nor subdued by the sudden misfortunes I face in life, no matter how tedious or painful they may seem at that moment.

One who doesn't rise is easily tamed and subdued because he cannot see the whole picture. From below, affliction always seem beyond resolution, but those who are positioned to rise are empowered as they catch a birds-eye-view. When God lifts one up, He elevates that mind to a spiritual plane that heals wounds and soothes troubled persons. It's imperative to keep in mind that afflictions felt down here are only temporary and by positioning oneself, God can lift that fragile spirit high above the pain and hurt until the storm passes over. There are far more intrinsic and extrinsic rewards to be derived from positioning oneself to rise than all the momentary bliss of instant gratification and retaliation.

When the pressures of this world get us down, we must position ourselves to soar high above those problems to look at the whole picture. One glance at the whole picture revitalizes us because the things that seemed overwhelming from below are like mere milestones from on high. Learning lessons from birds helps us soar to evade frustration and depression. For instance, an eagle can circle about in the sky without any detectable movement of its wings. Whenever the eagle wants to gain altitude, it soars to an area where there is a thermal updraft that will carry it upward without any attempt on its own.

Sometimes, people become easily overwhelmed with the cares of this life when troubles get them down quicker than a resolution can be made; they must learn to trust God with all their heart without leaning to their own understanding (Proverbs 3:5, 6). In that capacity, the updraft of God's Spirit can lift their souls upwards. Isaiah imposed four rewards for trusting God without leaning to our own understanding: renewed strength; mount up with wings like eagles; run and not be weary and walk and not faint (Isaiah 40:10). God has the power of a thermal updraft that will carry one upward without any attempt of his own. He can lift up enfeeble spirits above present and past burdens that try to propel them downwards. All one has to do when the pressures of life get him down is to make the decision to position himself to rise above it by letting go and allowing God. He can empower and elevate one's mind to a place of tranquility where hope, joy, peace and harmony can be attained despite the intensity of one's present circumstances.

To increase the reach towards greater glory, one must not only rise but also soar high in order to see the whole picture and find greater resolve. I've learned lessons from the birds that helped me to rise above difficulties and escape the consequences that would have been ascribed had I succumb to the temptation. Practice "soaring high."

When facing adversity one may desire to have temporal glory back and to attain this, one must position oneself to rise above past hurts or pain. Catching a birds-eye-view makes one see the whole picture with all its interrelating part. David caught a birds-eye-view and his enfeebled spirit was bolstered time and again. Through songs, worship and praise he positioned himself for greater glory. People who do not rise above what is past only see the little aggravating things that plague them in everyday life; those very things that propel them downward and block off their blessings. Trusting in God, He will empower all those that position themselves to rise like the birds, to view their troubles from a bird's-eye-view. With spiritual wings, one gets an extensive view of the entire problem from the sky. The higher one soars the bigger the picture one will see. Soaring like the eagle prevents one from jumping to conclusions, misunderstandings or judgments. Catching a birds-eye-view empowers one to see the whole picture and soaring higher helps one become an optimistic thinker, a positive leader or an enthusiastic follower. With a birds-eye-view, one can make decisions based on all the facts rather than mere speculations or assumptions. Beginning now, one can position oneself to catch a birds-eye-view.

One who taps into God's fountain of grace and mercy will find a sheltering spiritual wing that shields him from all harms and keeps his spirit from faltering. To rise, one has to visualize that he or she is special in God's sight for through His empowerment it is possible to rise above fears, limitations and doubts. This requires faith as Paul said, "Without faith, it is impossible to please God." Those who believe that "With God all things are possible" position themselves to rise high above problems and through their faith, God will lift their drooping spirit to extend their reach towards greater glory. "Those who see the invisible can do the impossible"

4. Practicing Peacemaking

Peacemaking is another key component that increases one's reach towards fuller glory. It is about living peaceably with all. Even though it is rather difficult to make peace with all types of personalities, it is a crucial aspect of increasing the reach towards greater glory and requires striving to perfect that mark.

A major aspect of peacemaking is laying aside all malice, guile, hypocrisies, envies and evil speaking (1 Peter 2:1). Some people have a difficult time being peacemakers because they are too proud to let others know that they are human enough to make mistakes. They would rather risk pushing aside others to feed their pride. We must all be cognizant of the fact that "God resisteth the proud, and giveth grace to the humble" (1 Peter 5:5 KJV). Instead of stalling the peacemaking process to hug false pride, we must understand that sometimes it's just a little weakness that needs to be made strong. By staying humble in God's sight, "He will lift you up" (1 Peter 5:6 The Clear Word).

Being hospitable to others is a crucial condition of peacemaking for 1 Peter 4:9 admonishes us to, "Use hospitality one to another without grudging" (KJV). 2 Peter 3:9 further warns that, "The Lord is not slack concerning his promise." Therefore, even though we cannot understand why it is necessary to follow some of God's precepts, it is imperative that we take Him at His word and do what is right to others because that matters to Him. Putting self aside helps make this process a much easier one to undertake. There is more to gain from accepting

God's promises that promotes peacemaking than by running or hiding, being defensive, becoming elusive or evading truths in an effort to conceal vulnerabilities.

Practicing peacemaking is more intense than just loving peace. Many times we feel that just by evading truths, sparing others feelings and not responding to a wrongful act that we are peacemakers, but there is a marked difference between peace lovers and peacemakers. Peace lovers do just about anything to make peace, even if it means compromising their values or God's law. Peacemakers are more concerned about doing what is right in the sight of God rather than pleasing man. Inevitably, when one seeks to do what is right in the sight of God, he automatically does what is best for his fellowmen. Peace is not the absence of turmoil but the stamina to maintain one's composure within a turbulent circumstance; seeking the best possible outcome in a stormy situation.

A striking feature of the covenant of peace is that God has made a provision for humanity to access His pardoning grace. God vows to be merciful to the unrighteous, but He does not dishonor His Law to show mercy to a pardoned sinner by suffering the Law to be defiled by iniquity. Each sinner that repents and confesses his sins will find pardon under the new Law for as many as receive Him, He promises to give them the power to become His very own. That is what makes glory within our reach. As we receive Christ by repentance and confession, our spirits will merge with His Will. As a result, we will receive power to forgive and become peacemakers. Only then can the robe of Christ's righteousness cover our sinful nakedness, causing us to do right and live gloriously.

Peace is a state of mind that is accomplished individually through oneness with our Creator. As the prophet says in Isaiah 26:3, 4, "You [LORD] will keep in perfect peace him whose mind is steadfast..." (NIV). To attain peace, we have to begin allowing our lives to change. As frail human beings, we can't purify our own hearts—only the Spirit of Holiness can. He has the power to transform lives, but before that happens, we have to believe Him and then accept the divine gift that He has imparted unto us. That's reaching! It would be much easier if after our lives are transformed we didn't have to continue to fight against evil. Since we do, we have to constantly rely on Christ—our highest source of power—to help us rise above sin and self while we maintain peace as we go through storms and pain. People who seek to extend their reach towards greater glory strive to become instrument of peace, as described in the following "Prayer of Saint Francis of Assisi" that is attainable if we let go and let God.

"Lord, make me an instrument of Your peace.
Where there is hatred let me sow love;
Where there is injury, pardon;
Where there is doubt, faith;.
Where there is despair, hope;

Where there is darkness, light;
And where there is sadness, joy.
O divine Master, grant that I may not so much seek
To be consoled as to console;
To be understood as to understand;
To be loved as to love.
For it is in giving that we receive;
It is in pardoning that we are pardoned;
And it is in dying that we are born to eternal life."

Earlier we learned that in this world, we have a choice to execute our free will to choose to do good or evil. One who is not a viable part of a solution is part of a problem because accepting the role of being a peacemaker, empowers us to:

- Love those who do us wrong, even our enemies.
- Be accountable for our brothers and sisters.
- Reach out to the poor and homeless.
- Love our neighbors as ourselves.
- Witness to the loss and wounded.
- Reconcile our differences.
- Share with those who are less fortunate.

5. Holding Daily Devotion

Holding daily devotion is an important component that positions one to extend the reach towards fuller glory. We are God's workmanship. That means, God is constantly trying to work on us to make us what He wants us to be, and the only way He can access us is if we tap into Him by staying in tune with Him daily. To position ourselves to do this, we must stay in daily devotion with God through prayer, study and praise; this helps us cultivate an understanding of His divine character that extends the reach for fuller glory. The bible says, "Study to show thyself approved unto God," "pray without ceasing" and "praise." If the language we use when coming into personal daily devotion with God reflects one of honesty, humility and a strong desire to honor and obey God, it will increase His stronghold on our lives and extend our reach towards fuller glory. Through daily devotion, we may have a closer walk with God; that will dictate how we walk, talk and treat each other. It teach us how to:

- Grow in our Christian walk
- Listen to the voice of the Holy Spirit
- Get wisdom to face the struggles of each new day
- Discern things rightfully
- Wait on God and be patient
- Obtain inner peace
- Lighten our heavy burden
- Find comfort and strength to do the impossible
- Increases our faith

Without the aid of the Holy Spirit, we are helpless as newborn babies. Spending time in daily devotion with God, sincerely and selflessly, desiring to change anything that's unlike Him and do faithfully the duties He has set forth each day puts us within glorious realms. Going to God with pure hearts that are desirous of bringing glory and honor to His name creates a connection between the Creator and us. It prepares us to live a God-filled life, which according to Titus 1:13—2:14 is to:

Speak out the things that make solid doctrine. Guide older men into a life of temperance, dignity and wisdom, into healthy faith, love and endurance. Guide older women into lives of reverence so they end up as neither gossip nor drunks, but as models of Goddesses. By looking at them, the younger women will know how to love their husbands and children, be virtuous and pure, keep a good house, be good wives... Also, guide young men to live disciplined lives. But mostly, show them all this by doing it ourselves, incorruptible in our teaching, and our words. Then, anyone who is dead set against us, when he finds nothing weird or misguided, might eventually come around... Then his good character will shine through his actions, adding luster to the teaching of our Savior God. God's readiness to give and forgive is now public. Salvation 's available to everyone! We are being shown how to turn our backs on a godless, indulgent life, and how to take on God-filled, God-honoring life. This new life is starting right now and is wetting our appetites for the glorious day when our great God and Savior, Jesus Christ, appears. (The Message).

For those who are unfamiliar or lacking of the benefits that are derived from having a life of daily devotion, I recommend beginning with the book of wisdom—Proverbs. This book contains the essence of biblical wisdom in practical terms. It provides common sense spiritual wisdom for every day living. However, the wisdom will be difficult, perhaps impossible, to put into practice unless one is actively positioning oneself through prayer to reach for fuller glory.

6. Optimism

The only thing barring us from having an optimistic outlook in life is a pessimistic mindset. By elevating our thoughts from a negative mindset to positive enthusiasm extends our reach towards greater glory. People who are optimistic tend to live longer, happier and more fulfilled lives. In this world, it is easier to have a negative outlook than a positive mindset because as we look at the people around us, the news and the things that transpire around us everyday, we visualize mentally a doctrine that the world is fundamentally evil. It is absolutely easy to fall into a pit of pessimism, for pessimism is so contagious that it spreads like an epidemic that is difficult to counteract. My formula for optimism is a tool I constructed to help discover new possible ways to overcome barriers in life and increase my reach towards greater glory. A careful inventory of past experience can help anyone who wants to take a proactive step to become more optimistic and successful.

My Formula For Optimism

> **MY FORMULA FOR OPTIMISM IS:**
> **=BREAKING + UP + THE + SICKNESS + OF +**
> **PESSIMISM**

Breaking up the sickness of pessimism is my formula for optimism; an antidote for the pessimism epidemic. It is not easy to practice the A, B, C's because the forces of evil are so prevalent in our world today. It is hard to stay focused on the positive when everywhere greater importance placed on the negative. A unique strategy I've taken to help attain an optimistic outlook is found within the formula. Because pessimism is an every day struggle for survival, one must see it as something that must be combated in order to recuperate from the long hold it has on one's life. Let's take a closer look:

<u>MY FORMULA FOR OPTIMISM =</u>

Build your character based on a good value system
Recognize talents, opportunities and strengths; let them conquer limitations
Empower yourself through prayer and the study of the word.
Acknowledge faults and mistakes, appreciate self and accept difference
Know what you stand for, then stand and be counted
Invigorate your mind, body and soul
Nurture your inner spirits
Grow in areas you could never have imagined
+
Unleash to your full potential
Plan for the future relentlessly, aspire and prepare for tough times ahead
+
Take kindly to wise counsel, especially that of elders
Help those in need without looking for compensation or applaud
Encourage those who are in need
+
Speak to people; be nice to everyone
Improve yourself continuously and inspire yourself to be adaptive change
Create a positive atmosphere to thrive in
Keep peace while taking time to remember the little blessings in life
Never give in to fear or doubt
Embrace your relationships with family, friends and spouse
Smile with people and if possible laugh at the little things around you
Sow good seeds and do good deeds
+
Overcome barriers, threats, challenges and limitations
Forgive those who trespass against you and forget the negative impact
+
Pray for strength to help you overcome lack, loss and limitations
Expect positive things and explore all options before making decisions
Stand up for what is right
Strive for excellence
Increase in wisdom and understanding
Meditate on God's word and keep a song in your heart
Identify yourself with positive people
Shun evil friends and choose your companionships with care.
Measure your success factor

To become optimistic, one has to start thinking more positively about oneself, others and the surrounding. It is not disputable that optimism is a difficult thing to do with all of the negativity, distress, frustrations, sadness and strife in the world around, but it takes a conscious effort to develop positive attitudes and keep positive thoughts, habits and feelings. One that has a pessimistic viewpoint has to do much more than trying to elevate his mindset from a negative outlook to positive enthusiasm. Elevating one's mindset from a negative outlook to a positive enthusiasm may be easy for some types of personalities, but it takes much practice for others. By elevating one's mindset from a negative outlook to positive enthusiasm, one chooses to let go of poor thoughts and attitudes that block everyday blessings. A great way to elevate one's mindset from a negative outlook to positive enthusiasm is through formulating good attitudes, thoughts and feelings about oneself and the world around her. This will improve the overall communication process and begin a network that allows one to share helpful information and increase understanding. Some effective ways to do this is through friendly attitudes, positive persuasion, asking questions when in doubt, getting answers to life's probing questions without becoming defensive or offensive and sharing one's personal experiences without imposing personal values on others. Practice does make better and gradually joy will begin to spring forth in a heart that makes a conscious effort to grow.

When a heart is full of joy and enthusiasm, life will become more meaningful. Good attitudes come from positive thinking. It enables one to be optimistic and leads to a more rewarding life in the face of adversities, doubt, grief and pain. It is possible to help someone else feel better or important by rewarding positive behaviors and ignoring negative behaviors; that's a good way to spread positive enthusiasm.

Despite all the trickery, drudgery and confusion in the world today, it is possible for one who has been a pessimist all through life to become positively enthusiastic. Regardless of how good one's attitude may be or how effectively one communicates with others, there'll always be reasons to succumb to a negative mindset; however, there are tips that may be helpful to help one improve his level of enthusiasm. To elevate one's thoughts from a negative outlook to positive enthusiasm you have to:

1. Develop a heightened relationship and tap into your highest source of power.
2. Always look for the good in yourself and others.
3. Build a healthy self-esteem, discard all thoughts of self-pity, get rid of that poor old me attitude and do something about your own situation.
4. Step outside yourself and get to know others just the way they are and not what you want to make them.
5. Receive every adversity positively, seeing trials and temptations as challenges that can be turned into blessings if approached enthusiastically.
6. Don't be quick to give up on dreams and goals that seem unattainable.
7. Give up judgmentalism, speculations and gossip that kill your inner spirit.

Keep in mind that the minute one lets up and allows one negative thought, attitude or feeling to foster, there will be a growth so fast that this individual may find it hard to come up for air before there is another and another. That is why it is imperative to guard the avenue of the soul,—your inner thoughts, from any form of pessimism. No one has the power to make one do something that he or she doesn't want to do, so stop blaming others. Instead:

- ♦ Choose being in a good mood over a bad mood.
- ♦ Choose being in a good mood even when something bad happens.
- ♦ Choose to learn from bad situations over becoming a victim of it.
- ♦ Every time someone comes complaining, choose to listen to his complaint and then point out the positive side of life.
- ♦ Anytime someone comes spread a little gossip, choose to rise above partaking in the subtle negative messages conveyed and suggest stop passing it along until talebearer knows the facts.
- ♦ Choose to always look on the positive side of life.

It takes discipline, determination, persistence and perseverance to elevate one's mindset from a negative outlook to positive enthusiasm. By practicing, one increases his or her reach towards greater glory. Taking a proactive approach to becoming optimistic improves one's self and increases one's reach towards greater glory.

7.   Increase with Wisdom and Understanding

Choosing a life that is in accordance with God's will helps us evade the suffering and consequences of wrong actions. Increased wisdom and understanding are crucial towards increasing the reach toward greater glory. Though some people suffer for varied reasons—unrelated to being lazy, sinful or back—some suffer because of their lifestyle choices. When people do not increase in wisdom and understanding, they'll make unwise decisions, causing them to heap unnecessary consequences.

There are many benefits that are derived from increasing in wisdom and understanding. Solomon gives us directives in the book of Proverbs about how to get wisdom and understanding and live wisely. To position oneself for growth and/or progress one must have a good command of wisdom and understanding. To understand what wisdom constitutes examine the following.

<u>Characteristics Of The Wise (See Proverbs 1).</u>

(1) They receive instruction of wisdom, justice, judgement and equity
(2) Give subtilty to the simple
(3) Will hear and increase learning
(4) Attain unto wise counsels

Not only did Solomon give instructions about how to increase in wisdom and understanding, but tells what is needed to become discrete. Diligence is an essential characteristic. Proverbs 2: 4, 23 instructs us to, "Keep your heart with all diligence;

for out of it are the issues of life." Proverbs 2:11-18 also outlines some reasons why we should have discretion. In summary, discretion preserves and understanding keeps or sustains. Here are some things that discretion preserves and understanding keeps from:

Six things discretion preserves and understanding keep us from:

(1) Delivers from the way of evil men who walk in the ways of darkness
(2) Delivers from those whose ways are crooked
(3) Strange women who flatters with their lips
(4) They that are froward things
(5) Those who rejoice to do evil
(6) Those who delight in the forwardness of the wicked

Despite all the knowledge we acquire through institutes of higher learning and all the experiences we have in life, increased wisdom and understanding is limited outside of fearing God. Here is a suggested plan for increasing in wisdom and understanding.

(1) Receive the words of God and hide his commandments with you
(2) Incline your ears unto wisdom
(3) Apply your heart unto understanding
(4) Cry after knowledge
(5) Lift up your voice for understanding

Increasing in wisdom and understanding calls for reaching, which positions one to extend the reach towards greater glory. Proverbs 2:9 advocates that only by doing the above things can one understand righteousness, judgement and equity. Only God can give wisdom and understanding to the righteous. We have to start thinking strategically. The time has come for us to stop relying on our own strength and intellect to give the kind of wisdom that is needed to get ahead. We cannot spend a number of hours investing in things that will have no value to us in terms of spiritual, physical, mental, emotional or social growth. Regardless of whether it is material possessions, friendships, relationships, assets or financial investments if what we hold dear is not going to make us grow in every true sense of the word, we have to give it up. If God is not in it, all of it will soon crumble before our face much like the Twin Towers did on September 11, 2001 and the stock market continues to do to this day.

Of all the things we are focusing on, GOD must be put first in our lives if we are positioning to become a success. It is His leading that empowers us to act wisely and think diligently. That way, in times of troubles we will have the inner strengths and character, financial and emotional, the physical and spiritual aptitude to move ahead amid all obstacles. A mindset like this causes one to run and never get weary, walk and not faint.

Things that extend our reach of glory bring happiness into our lives and happiness always tends to come through doors we didn't even realize we had opened. From happiness flows the wellspring of joy, peace, harmony and hope. To attain this, we have to begin positioning ourselves by reaching out today. If we think this is impossible, here's what Martin Luther had to say, "God created the world out of nothing, and as long as we are nothing, He can make something out of us." If God can work with me to extend my reach, he can help anyone else.

Chapter 10

OVERCOMING PAINFUL SITUATIONS

Since the loss of full glory, humanity has been faced with painful situations, but many do not know what it takes to overcome nonetheless what it means to get through barriers to win the victory. Overcoming pain calls for reaching for greater glory. Oftentimes, we react in undesirable ways to things that haunt us; instead of reaching for greater glory, we put ourselves in danger of not growing or ever overcoming. One way that people react to painful situations that is a detriment to overcoming entails sweeping the problem under the rug then pretend it didn't happen and hope that it goes away. However, the only thing sweeping problems under the rug creates a rotten mildew ready to raise its stench that is more of an agony than the initial problem actually had been. Murphy's Law specifies that, *"left to themselves, things tend to go from bad to worse."* Only those who understand that overcoming is an ongoing process—an uphill battle that must be faced each day can get through painful situations with their dignity while avoiding future mildew problems.

Overcoming calls for stepping out of self: pride and selfishness. We can then face the problem head on, so that we can learn from our past to erase the past and reach for greater glory. Our objective should never be to avoid the storm or finding ways to get out of it before we should. Going through the storm allows God to pass over us and touch us with His empowering presence. As we gracefully go through storms and pain in our lives, God passes through the tempest to bring calm, comfort and peace. When we choose to stay in the storm, the tempest will not overtake us, for God is in the midst of it. According to the psalmist, *"He will not be moved neither will He suffer our foot to be moved"* (121:3). Because we are made in His image and empowered by His Spirit, we are capable of regenerating ourselves despite the storm. Yet, to win the ultimate victory, we have to stay in the storm. Like the Hebrew boys, we need the faith of Jesus to step into the storm and the fire to save us from sudden destruction. What we have to remember is that if God is on our side when we are going through the storms and the pain, the tempest will not overwhelm us. The only thing that saved the Hebrew people from the fate of the Egyptians was the blood that was sprinkled over their door. If they had not obeyed and walked by faith, they would have been consumed like all the others that perished that day. When we bear our crosses with grace through the storm and pain, God will send divine deliverance to protect us.

None of us are immune to pain or suffering no matter how hard we try. We all are equally vulnerable and susceptible to the painful situations, and it will continue to be that way until we get back to our glorious home, Eden. However, there are some temporal glories—peace, joy, hope and harmony that we can receive while in this world of sin but not of ourselves, for it is a gift that God reserves for those who follow after righteousness.

We all have to endure our share of pain and sorrows in life but as we reach for greater glory, each day we can look forward to facing the world with all of its new possibilities and uncertainties. Natural and initial responses to troubles cause us to become anxious, stressed and overwhelmed, but by allowing our inert spiritual abilities to kick in for us, we can get some help while going through the storm process, without trying to escape or pass over it.

Overcoming Adversities

The whole world can identify with one adversity, the attack of September 11, but not too many people know how to truly overcome those mechanical responses to feel joyful and hopeful. When the walls of the World Trade Center came tumbling down, many ran to churches to pray, but I am not so sure how many really got what they went looking for. What we have to understand is that there is no preacher nor is there any physical church structure, building, that can pick up the broken, empty pieces of our lives.

The only true test to determine if one is an overcomer is one's willingness to face his or her greatest fears and endure unavoidable adversities. When faced with adversities, we can take advantage of our inner strengths, putting them to work so that we can overcome our internal weaknesses. Similarly, we can utilize our external opportunities to help us overcome our external threats. We'll need all the strength we can get when unexpected difficulties arise; letting go of the old baggage is helpful— especially when it belongs to someone else. An old baggage is anything that may weigh us down, hold us back or retard our progress. When we leave old baggage behind, we leave room for fresh courage, new strengths and revitalized energies all which give us new beginnings to fight our next adversity with all our might. If we can recognize the plea of the Spirit that lies within even for a brief moment, we may recognize that God's light is still shining our way. God is willing and able to hear us when we call, catch us when we fall, carry us through the storms and pain to keep us from stumbling again.

We all hit rock bottom sometimes when Satan steals our joy, peace and hope by paralyzing us with fear, but we can reclaim what Satan has stolen from us by reaching out to God. We position ourselves by reaching out by faith to Jesus, for He knows just what to do. God can drive out fear, so we cannot continue living the same way we did before. We have to shun evil things and people that tell us only what they think we want just to boost our confidence. To overcome the enemy, we must rely on God's power, not our own. Positioning ourselves through God's power, we can overcome this web of lies and deception that Satan has set to trap us. The Bible admonishes, "resist the devil, he will flee from you" (James 4:7). Letting go moves God to de-tangle us from Satan's booby traps.

Regardless of what force of evil avails, God specializes in making righteous dreams come true, and He can do what seems impossible by driving out fear when we call Him. Relying on God, we gain renewed strength as He raises us up out of the pit. When He does, we have to raise our standards boldly so that Satan cannot permeate our minds or work his way into our heart to cut off our divine blood flow. As God works on us to create within us a clean heart, a right spirit and a transformed mind, we have to surrender fully to Him. Building on the rock, Christ Jesus, can merit us the victory to overcome, for in Him lies all our strength. The Bible says that "at the name of Jesus every knee shall bow and every tongue will confess." To survive the test, we must face adversities head on, cultivate good characteristics and continuously improve so that our foot is not moved; we do not have to run or hide, go with the tide or get left behind when the enemy comes in like a flood.

Attributes and Benefits of an Overcoming Spirit

There are various indications of an overcoming spirit. A soul that has overcome adversities has a progressive, upward and forward moving, sentiment. As frail human beings, none of us has the power to empower ourselves but are empowered through the Spirit of God that lives within us. If we try on our own to become overcomers, we will continue stumbling downward into the paths of Satan as oppose to an upward, forward progress led by our divine Redeemer. In our own strength, we cannot be overcomers without the power of the indwelling Spirit. Attributes of an overcoming spirit are echoed in Jesus' sermon on the mount—the Beatitudes: "*Love your enemies, bless them that curse you, do good to them that hate you, and pray for them which despitefully use you, and persecute you;*" and the **REASON** *"that ye may be the children of your Father which is in heaven..."* (Matthew 6:44,45 KJV). As forceful as that is, Matthew 5 gives us a complete stance on the attributes of an overcoming spirit. The table below summarizes those attributes that position us to receive greater glory as well as indicate that of one who has an overcoming spirit.

ATTRIBUTES OF AN OVERCOMING SPIRIT	PRACTICAL MEANINGS
Poor in spirit	Feeling that we have nothing good in ourselves and rely on God.
They that mourn	We are so grief-stricken that we cry out in agony of spirit.
Meek	Those of us who have seen our own helplessness and cry out to God as a hopeless sinner.
Hunger and thirst after righteousness	A deep yearning to become more like Christ in character.
Merciful	Those of us who remain patient while treated unjustly, care for those around us and forgive those who do us wrong.
Pure in heart	Guarding the avenue of our souls by nurturing and controlling our inner spirit: emotions, thoughts, actions, attitude, mind and will; giving them totally over to God, so He can come in to cleanse us and free us from sin.
Peacemakers	It is *not* evading a problem but facing it, dealing with it and conquering it to become a servant of God and lover of others; crucifying our willful nature and dying to self.
Persecuted for righteousness sake	Those of us who become physical, social or emotional martyrs because we stand up for what's right by godly principle.
Men revile, persecute, and say all manner of evil against falsely.	Those of us who get ostracized by lies of others because we are willing and determined to do what is right.

It is imperative that we are aware that Christ called people in all these categories BLESSED. We must also keep in mind that when Jesus said, "blessed," he means happy so that we can fulfill our duty in this world—to become the salt of the earth and light bearers. If we overcome our adversities and bear our crosses with grace, we will get some rewards here and eternally.

Benefits of an Overcomer

There are many benefits to be derived from an overcoming spirit. Our character is revealed in times of crisis. We either bear our crosses with grace as we stand up for what is right to follow after righteousness or follow the destructive path to sin and evil. Our attitudes in times of crisis reflects who we really are. As we all face adversities, the piety and grace we previously portrayed slowly tends to fade as we react or respond mechanically to the adversities we face. Unless we possess the attributes displayed in the table below, we cannot feel the intrinsic/extrinsic rewards and blessings that are assigned to each characteristic.

ATTRIBUTES OF AN OVERCOMING SPIRIT	REWARDS	SOURCE
Poor in spirit	Inherit the kingdom of heaven	Matthew 5: 3
They that mourn	Shall be comforted	5:4
Meek	Inherit the earth	5:5
Hunger and thirst after righteousness	Be filled	5:6
Merciful	Obtain mercy	5:7
Pure in heart	Shall see God	5:8
Peacemakers	Called the children of God	5:9
Persecuted for righteousness sake,	Kingdom of heaven	5:10
Men revile, persecute, and say all manner of evil against falsely	Reward is in heaven	5:12

While going through the storms and the pain, we must remember not to allow the mechanical factors to work for us adversely, and if they do, it is important that we make a quick recovery. As painful as a tragedy may be, God is working things out for our good, and we have to bear our crosses with compassion and grace by staying in the storm and the heat until God lifts the yoke of our burdens from our lives. To do this, we must seek God while He may be found, having faith and trusting Him where we cannot trace Him. Anything else is not good enough in God's sight. It is crucial that we develop an up close and personal relationship with Christ and seek Him until we find Him because He is searching for us and will come through for us. Despite what Satan or any of his agents tell us or tries to do to us, we have to understand that God never puts more on us than we can bear (1 Corinthians 10:13). We have to believe that all those rewards and blessings that Christ promised are ours if we reach out and claim them, but they are inaccessible to us if we are not able to overcome. Those who overcome will be granted a seat with Christ in His throne because even as He has also overcome and is set down with His Father at the throne. Therefore, Christ admonishes us to be an overcomer and *"He that hath an ear, let him hear what the Spirit saith unto the churches"* (Revelations 3:21).

Chapter 11

GETTING THROUGH UNEXPECTED STORMS AND PAIN

For some of us, it is easy to get out of a sticky situation when we know it is coming but our greatest test of faith as frail human beings is the challenge of getting through unexpected storms and pain. Everyday, we plan our lives but not very often we plan or prepare ourselves for the unexpected. When the unexpected comes, we get taken off guard and even the most religious among us can lose our bearings. One who gets through unexpected storms and pain has to position oneself and reach to receive greater glory.

The experience of losing three significant males in my life within three years exemplified unexpected storms and intense pain, but how I got through that storm and pain proved to be a necessary challenge that strengthened me. Up until a few years ago I was lost in the rags of my sins and, like my ancestors, found myself wandering away from the paths of righteousness. The farther I wandered, the more I lost the glory. So, I began running and hiding like many others from my Creator and those whom I love, fearing that they would find out who I really was and condemn me. As I ran and hid, I further displeased God by neglecting my moral obligation to others and not giving back to the Creator. I realized that I was living outside of His glory.

Suddenly, I began to discover that the reason why humanity suffers so profusely at the hands of each other and the hands of the enemy of souls, Satan, is that we have walked in our own willful ways and have become lost in the darkness. Not lost because God is unmerciful or uncaring but lost because we have chosen a course where the light of God's glory cannot thrive. That is why wrong seems right. Every time I sinned: lied, cheated, stole, backbitten, gossiped, hated, scorned et cetera, I felt the guilt, shame, pain, dis-harmony and gloom associated with the loss of glory. Before I reached for the light, I wandered farther into the forest where the weeds, thorns and thistles in my character began to choke out the good seeds, the fruits of the Spirit: love, joy peace, longsuffering, tenderness, kindness, mercy, meekness and faith. This was a miserable state to find myself in.

As a part of humanity, I had to learn patience instead of being too quick witted, for I encountered that in God's own time He will make all things beautiful. At times, I get overly enthused when I see others going through similar situations that desire victory because I can share my tools of success for victory. However, sharing such tools don't always go so well. As flawed human beings, sometimes we take offense to others who try to help because we do not see the help the way it was intended. We tend to see it in our natural eyes and that imperfect visual makes us see it as pointing out our weaknesses rather than trying to empower us. That is what sin does to us, it blinds us to the realities, but God can help us put things back into perspective if we reach out to Him.

Anytime I am going through a painful situation I usually take a brief look back to learn from previous storms that I overcame because history has a way of teaching me. I have learned one thing in life: God cannot reach me until I look within myself to see where I went wrong first, then make amends and reach out to Him. That gives me the courage to face whatever obstacles I experience. I find that the more faith I exhibit, the more God answers my prayers and delivers me from all misery and despair. I have also discovered other equipment to aid the committed soldier: focusing, smiling, laughing, singing, and accepting.

Tips For Triumph, While Going Through Storms and Pain

1. **FOCUS:** Keeping my heart and mind focused on God helps me get through the storms and pain. I manage to keep my heart and mind stayed on God throughout my daily routine. Focusing on God each moment helps me to balance my life and put all my other duties into perspective. As I do this, I find that God is easily accessible to me when I need Him. While going through a difficulty, I keep my mind focused on God's strength for the day. His strength provides me with rest for the weary and light for the day. I feel confident that I can do all things, including overcoming major obstacles and handling disappointments gracefully. Focusing makes it easier for me to tap into Him.

    I can never focus enough. I desire to always be aware of His ever-present desire for my good. Focus requires that I guard the avenues of my soul from evil communication, deception, pride, greed, lust, and any form of contamination or sin. It is easy to become lured into a not so glorious environment when surrounded by people who are not growing or conscious of their wrong doings. When drawn away, the Bible tells us to be sober and vigilant and admonishes me to shun evil companions for "evil communications corrupt good manners" (1 Corinthians 15:33 KJV). Instead of engaging with people who are unwise, the Apostle Paul admonishes that we focus and, "Awake to righteousness and sin not; for some have not the knowledge of God" (Vs.34). Hosea 4:6 reveals that some perish for a lack of knowledge, not because they never heard of Christ or are not aware of what is right but because of ignorance and indulgence. When I know what God expects of me, focusing on Him is easy. When I don't know what He expects of me, focusing on Him is a necessity.

My hardest struggle comes when facing friends or loved ones in circumstances that compromise godly standards, for it is difficult to face those I love, confront those I care about or make a decision to isolate myself from any association with them in order not to become enticed. However, by staying focused and standing on Christ's righteousness, not debating about the Word of God, I am able to stand knowing that the payoff is far greater. By focusing, I listen to my voice of reasoning inside and even if I risk losing my loved ones and friendships, I have to stand firm in order to merit God's favor.

2. **SMILE**: Every time storms arise, I smile the dark clouds away. Because most people in the world are not truly happy, smiling can be taken in the wrong way, but we have to learn to smile with, not at, others for it can make this world a better place. Smiling is a good way I improve my human relationships. A sincere smile can arouse feelings of goodwill with fewer muscles; it takes 27 muscles to frown and only 14 to smile. If I can't find anything to smile about, I start thinking of the storms God brought me through and that's enough to make me smile. So take heed to this poem and "catch a smile" then pass it along to someone else.

<u>Catch a smile</u>
Smiling is infectious,
You catch it like the flu!
When someone smiled at me today,
I started smiling too!

I passed around the corner
And someone saw my grin,
And when he smiled, I realized
I passed it on to him!

I thought about that smile
And I realized its worth—
A single smile just like mine
Could travel 'round the earth!

So, if you feel a smile begin,
Don't leave it undetected…
Let's start an epidemic quick,
And get the world infected!!!
Author Unknown

3. **LAUGHTER:** I make laughter my best medicine while going through storms and pain. I've discovered that laughter has healing properties, for it prevents heartache and pain as well as restores my joy. Ecclesiastes 3:1 says, *"To everything there is a season, and a time for every purpose under the heaven,"* and I see too many pass up on the opportunity to have a good laugh and become drab and unhealthy as their body, mind and soul gradually begins to die. Solomon said in Proverbs 17:22, *"A merry heart doeth good like medicine: but a broken spirit drieth the bones."* When I am filled with anxious cares and negative thoughts that overwhelm me, I find real joy in the pleasures of the little everyday things in life. Laughter relaxes me. Looking at the simple things in life, I always find reasons to laugh. While I go through hardships, I find good reasons to laugh. Jorjette, a good friend of mine, when she was doing her Doctorate in Pharmacology, often turned to me when she needed to relieve some stress; oftentimes without any effort, I would get her to really laugh from deep inside; this would get me to laugh in response. Somehow, I never had to rehearse or dig deep to find a good laugh because deep down within I don't take life too seriously and laughing comes naturally. Proverbs 15:13 "A merry heart maketh a cheerful

countenance: but by sorrow of the heart is the spirit is broken." My laxity about the little everyday things and the ability to laugh at myself is always enough. I marvel at uptight and unhappy people, for there is a natural cure—laughter. With a good belly laugh, everything that can be worked out seems to get worked out. Laughter makes me feel happy and free as it relieves my anxieties. We can release all our negative energies through a warm laughter.

4. **SING:** Keeping a song in my heart helps me get through my storms and pain. With God as my source of highest power and the driving force behind my motives, it is easier to keep a song in my heart. Sometimes, I don't even think about what song I am going to sing, for God puts within my heart a melody as he whispers, "Fear not, I am with thee" while going through storms and pain. When I sing confidently to give honor and praise, God will protect and give me more reasons to sing. With a song in my heart, I can find unexplainable tranquility inside while the storm rages without.

5. **ACCEPT IT AND MOVE ON:** When bad things happen in my life, I am not alone, but sometimes it makes me feel uneasy when I have little or no control over it and that's okay if I can just accept that it happened and move on. The way I accept the storm is best illustrated by Dale Carnegie, *"First ask yourself: What is the worst thing that can happen? Then prepare to accept it. Then Proceed to improve on the worst."* After doing everything to avoid painful situations, if they still occur, I stand

for what is right and move on. By weighing all of my options before making a decision, I give myself a chance to listen to my voice of reasoning and pray about it before coming to a final conclusion. I give myself ample time to see the storm from different perspectives. When I move on, I am determined never to look back unless God brings me to a place of consciousness after preparing and signaling me to go back. However, when God sends me back to a situation that He initially pulled me away from, it is not for the same purpose that got me there to begin with. His purpose for me is to reach for greater glory.

Being in the storm has its dark side, for at times my spirit gets low and my thoughts get dreary, but I know that as quickly as I reach for greater glory and cry out, "Lord, lift me up! I want to go higher in thee" that He will reach down and rescue me. I realize many times that God does not make things come as easily for me as they do for others because He does not want me to live aloft on the mountainside. Instead, He picked out humble valleys for me so that He can lead me beside still waters to restore my soul. It is apparent to me that it is in the midst of the storms that I form my closest alliance with God and that is where I find comfort, rest and strength to carry on.

Instead of seeing my difficulties as a threat or a repercussion, I quickly remind myself that this world is not my home, and as I am trying to find my way back to my glorious home, I may have to endure some hardship. While I am in transition here, I am cognizant that I'm lurking on enemy territory and have to make the best of the experiences here. No matter how difficult the paths I have to take, I know that with God all things are possible. I have the hope for a victory that one day, humanity—the seeds of Adam and Eve, will have the victory if we reach for greater glory we along with Adam and Eve will be able to re-enter and inhabit our rightful home. There we will bask in the sunshine of God's eternal glory and with the ransomed will sing the song of Moses and the lamb and tell the story of how we have overcome. I am longing for such a day and that keeps me hopeful, joyful, peaceful and looking for the blessed hope. As I reach for greater glory, I find focusing, smiling, laughing, singing and accepting help keep me anchored on the paths of righteousness even though I may have to walk alone. This anchoring serves as a means of deliverance through any storm and keeps me reaching for greater glory.

Chapter 12

DELIVERANCE—OURSECRETHIDING PLACE

As frail human beings, we all find ourselves in messy circumstances, at one point in our lives or another, and we need deliverance—a secret hiding place—from our painful situation. Whether those situations are caused by our own negligence, our waywardness or an unexpected storm, when we find ourselves in such dilemmas that threatens our joy, peace, hope or harmony we quickly look for a secret hiding place—a place to hide until the storm passes over. Usually, we turn to seek refuge and find comfort in some source of strength we deem higher than ours. However, not all people tap into that main source from where true deliverance is derived to calm their fears, dispel their doubts and to quickly restore them back to glorious living. Only those who tap into their source of highest power by reaching for greater glory are delivered and find a hiding place where their distressed souls can once again love as it finds joy, peace, hope and harmony.

God is our Deliverer—our secret hiding place. True deliverance comes when God provides a shelter in the time of storm for those who will position themselves and reach beyond their present and past painful circumstances to Him for the greater glory. We know that we are delivered even when going through the storm of hardship. When God is sheltering us from a painful situation, He does not necessarily take us from the physical environment that's a choice we have to make, but by positioning ourselves He delivers us from the negative impact by giving hope and restoring joy, peace and harmony quickly.

Whether we are prepared or not, unexpected storms will come and since September 11, 2001, we all know what that can mean. However, when the storms of life are raging and the billows are tossing, our faith may be shaken, but our dreams and hopes do not have to become shattered, for if we abide in Him, God will shelter us from storms that encompass us. In Psalm 27:5, David promises that in the time of trouble God will hide us in His pavilion, in the secret place of His tabernacles, and set us upon a rock so that our head are lifted up above our enemies. Also, Nahum 1:5 assures us that the LORD has His way in the whirlwind and in the storms. Amazingly, the biggest clouds we go through are like mere dust at His feet. This is a side of God that the enemy does not want us to get to know because He wants us to keep on running and hiding in terror and fear until we miss our temporal glory and lose out on ultimate glory. God has empowered us so that even devils are subject to us through His name (Luke 10:17). That is why Satan is so hostile against us. He wants to keep us so bogged down with despair that we fail to recognize our true authority on this earth.

Special blessings and deliverance are available when we trust God. When storms of doubt gather and winds of strife begin to grow, we must not fear because the angel of the Lord encamps round about them that fear him, and He delivers them. As did David, we must *"Taste and see that the Lord is good"* (Psalm 34:7,8). There is no need to run or hide when God is our hiding place. When going through storms of pain, feelings of fear and darkness will soon disappear as the presence of God is felt. Walking on with love in our hearts moves God to shelter, hide and deliver us.

Deliverance is ours if we just believe and have faith. Whenever we need a shelter in the times of storm, there is a firm foundation; whose builder and maker is God. If we build our treasures on the Rock of Ages, then when the storm comes, our house will withstand the environmental elements. However, if we build it on the quicksand of this earthly empire, the house will fall. In the Rock of Ages, we can take comfort and receive deliverance amid the pestilence. When God calls us to go through deep waters, He is positioning us to receive greater glory and will not allow our rivers of sorrow to overflow without throwing out a lifejacket. If faced with fiery trials along the pathway, positioning oneself allow God's grace to be enough to kindle the fires so the flames may not hurt us but consume our dross and refine us like gold. Leaning on God for repose in times of trouble positions us, for He will never forsake us even while we are being shaken because the Lord is our deliverer!

Accepting the King of Glory as He comes into our lives brings us together in oneness and aligns us to receive our temporal glory—peace, joy, hope and harmony with each other. There is a force that lies within us that derives its power from the King of glory; it gives us power to rise above the past as well as those little everyday things that get in our way. This force is so strong that it causes us to love even those who do us wrong. When the power of God lives and reigns in a life, all trace of sin and darkness must be faced and then managed. When the King of glory abounds in us, He fills our every longing, takes away sin and sadness, frees us from bondage of storms then causes us to walk in the newness of life. That is how we regain temporal glory and can lead to ultimate glory.

Acts of terrorism, natural disasters and untimely deaths and sudden tragedy are unforeseen storms that often strike without giving any warning. The shock, fear and feelings of outrage felt when such calamity strikes are usually overwhelming. It usually leaves us feeling helpless, doubtful and in a state of abandonment that leads to hopelessness if we do not have a refuge to hide in. Amid devastation, loss and dismay, we must rest assured that God is our very present help in times of trouble. He is always near and will not leave nor forsake those who put their trust in Him for God reaches out with loving watch care when we are in despair. In His presence we find comfort, hope and assurance that we can draw strength from to begin rebuilding our lives. As we rebuild our lives after unforeseen storms leave us feeling dismayed, the strength and comfort we derive from reaching for greater glory can help us rebuild and strengthen our communities. Trusting in the Lord with all our hearts, we can reach out for help and find His arms open wide to renew our strength and restore our joy. A great place to find deliverance, safety and shelter when things suddenly go wrong is in the shadow of God's wings. Rest assured that God understands the fears, anger and anxiety that we go through. As we begin to rebuild our lives, God will take care of us and in times of trouble His love is sure. By reaching out to

Him and leaning on His Word, God will be our shelter and our strength. In His time, He makes everything beautiful and new so begin reaching for greater glory.

Reaching For Greater Glory

Why grope in this dark world sad and depressed
With our hearts bowed in sorrow and spirits oppressed,
When our souls can feel happy and securely rest;
For while walking with the King of glory, we'll be blest.

Those years I spent in vanity and pride
A state where God's Spirit just could not chide,
For where sin's fetter abound Satan had me bound;
And the world could not help us and no comfort found.

Now that I am walking with my Savior and King
I have a new purpose and a good reason to sing,
And like the birds in the sunbeams of spring;
I can echo God's praises and glad tidings bring.

For those where are downcast and weary of strife
Open up to the King of Glory and allow Him to enter your life,
For joy, peace, hope and harmony salvation will bring;
And reaching for greater glory, you'll
bask in the sunlight of the King.

For in the heart of my King there's enough love to shelter you
A love that's deep, kind, pure, tender and true,
So, why be broken, lonely, sad, tempted or for friendship cry;
When within the realm of glory, there's excessive supply.
Aminga D. Burton-Bracy

ABOUT THE AUTHOR

Aminga Burton-Bracy is a Doctoral Candidate currently working on completing her PhD in Organizational Psychology. Her dissertation title is, *Servant Leadership's Role: Examining the Relationship between Organizational Support and Organizational Commitment on Turnover Intentions*. Aminga is currently launching her consulting business. She worked for Southern Union Conference of SDA, an international faith-based organization, for almost 13 years in the Public Affairs and Religious Liberty (PARL) Department and ACS/Disaster Response for the last three years. Aminga holds a Masters of Arts degree in Organizational Management and a Bachelor of Science degree in Business Administration, specializing in Administrative Services. She is a dedicated wife and mother. Aminga is from an entrepreneurial family and got her early start in the Antigua where she was born, a British subject. Despite her busy schedule, Aminga finds time to volunteer for the DeKalb County CASA as a Court Appointed Special Advocate for Children as well as a youth counselor for the Atlanta Berean Crusaders Pathfinder Club. As a Master Guide, Aminga has dedicated her life to serving youth in this generation and works for the betterment of society.

Seeing God as her highest source of power, Aminga believes the response of a godly heart has an outward manifestation: "do justly, love mercy, and walk humbly with God" (Micah 6:8). She adapts this as a principle part of her personal worldview and strives to uphold it in all her dealings.

ENDNOTE

Introduction

Sternberg, R. J.; Trotter, K. & Swartwood, M. (2000). Lifespan: A multimedia introduction to human development. Wadsworth Cengage Learning.

Chapter 2

Hawthorne, N. (2000). Smith, J. & Clifford J. (Eds.) Young Goodman Brown. In Making Literature Matter: An Anthology for Readers and Writers. Boston: Bedford/St. Martins. 2

Hughes, Langston; Mullane, D., Ed. (1993). *Harlem is Crossing the Danger Water*, 508. Anchor Books/ Doubleday: NY1

Russell, F., A. (2002). Can't Wait to get Home. *Regional Voice Magazine, RV2-01*; 112. Silver Springs, MD. 3

Chapter 5

Anonymous (1983). Prince of Peace Control My Will. Review and Herald Publishing Association. Hagerstown, MD. (SDA Hymnal, 514). 1

Chapter 7

Trusty, J (2002). Week of Prayer Sermon on Generations.1

Chapter 9

Atkinson, R. L., Atkinson, R. C., Smith, E.E. & Bem, D. J. (1990). *Introduction to Psychology*, 514. Harcourt Brace Jovanovich Publishers: Orlando, FL.[1]

Hugo, Victor. (n.d.). Retrieved from www.brainy Quote. com.[2]